COLLEGE GRAD
SEEKS FUTURE

COLLEGE GRAD
SEEKS FUTURE

Turning Your Talents,

Strengths, and Passions

into the Perfect Career

Howard R. Greene, M.A., M.Ed.,
and Matthew W. Greene, Ph.D.

 ST. MARTIN'S GRIFFIN ⚏ NEW YORK

COLLEGE GRAD SEEKS FUTURE. Copyright © 2010 by Howard R. Greene and Matthew W. Greene. All rights reserved. Printed in the United States of America. For information, address St. Martin's Press, 175 Fifth Avenue, New York, N.Y. 10010.

www.stmartins.com

Book design by Maura Rosenthal / MSpace

Library of Congress Cataloging-in-Publication Data

Greene, Howard, 1937–
    College grad seeks future : turning your talents, strengths, and passions into the perfect career / Howard R. Greene and Matthew W. Greene.—1st ed.
         p. cm.
    ISBN 978-0-312-31542-9
    1. Vocational guidance. 2. Career development. 3. College graduates—Employment. I. Greene, Matthew W., 1968– II. Title.
    HF5381.G85585 2009
    650.14—dc22

2009011938

First Edition: May 2010

10 9 8 7 6 5 4 3 2 1

CONTENTS

PREFACE

THE MYTH OF THESEUS AND ARIADNE

> **clew** *or* **clue** 'klü *n* **1** : a ball of thread, yarn, or cord **2** *usu ue* : something that guides through an intricate procedure or maze of difficulties; *specif* : a piece of evidence that leads one toward the solution of a problem
>
> —*WEBSTER'S NEW COLLEGIATE DICTIONARY*,
> SPRINGFIELD, MA: G. & C. MERRIAM CO., 1979

GREEK MYTHOLOGY TELLS US THAT Theseus, hero of Athens, traveled to Crete alongside a group of young Athenians destined for sacrifice to the Minotaur, the dreaded half-man, half-bull creature dwelling in the Labyrinth beneath King Minos's palace. Theseus, dismayed by the annual tribute demanded by King Minos, volunteered to join the group in hopes of facing and killing the Minotaur, thus ending the reign of terror visited on his city as a result of Athens's role in the death of Minos's son.

Arriving in Crete, Theseus prepared to enter the Minotaur's lair, a cunning maze constructed by the famed builder Daedalus. Before doing so, Theseus was visited by Ariadne, the daughter of King Minos. Having fallen in love with Theseus, she offered to help him defeat the Minotaur and find his way out of the Labyrinth if he would return with her to Athens and make her his queen. He agreed.

Ariadne then provided Theseus with a sword and, most famously, a ball of Thread, or clew, which he could unravel at the entrance to the maze and follow to his freedom. This ball of thread, perhaps silk, perhaps gold, perhaps plain twine or yarn, allowed Theseus the means with which to find his path. Entering the maze with his companions, Theseus defeated the Minotaur. He then followed Ariadne's Thread back through the Labyrinth to reach his goal of returning to Athens with his companions.

Ariadne left Crete with Theseus, but never made it to Athens with him. There is disagreement about what happened to her along the way. She may have been left on the island of Naxos at the request of the God Dionysus, who coveted her for himself. She may have been put to death by Artemis on the island of Dia. She may have taken her own life. In any case, her role in the Theseus legend is not forgotten, and the concept of following a Thread to find a way through a maze, to solve a problem, to look for a set of clues to guide one's way, remains an enduring metaphor.

PROLOGUE

HOW FREQUENTLY DO YOU USE or hear the phrase, "I haven't got a clue!"? Perhaps you use it flippantly, or fervently. But where did this phrase originate? As with much of today's colloquial English, it originated in the ancient Greek and European past.

We believe that everyone has a Thread that is consistent through his or her life, and which connects personal choices, successes, and progress. More likely there are even series of Threads, or clues, that have come together and over time have woven your personal tapestry. This book is about discovering and following these Threads. The labyrinth you're in is a complex maze of opportunities, constraints, and expectations you face as a college student or graduate.

Each of you has made seemingly small as well as big decisions on the basis of your instincts or specific interests, talents, skills, and emotional and social needs. Over the course of your lifetime, these decisions will help you to choose your life's work. Consider the choices of friends, school courses, extracurricular activities, summer jobs, camps, and travel. Start with the college you chose, where you have made friendships, joined extracurricular groups and social clubs, selected an academic major, volunteered, and enjoyed off-campus programs and summer experiences. The options that you have avoided in all of these areas (out of a sense of dislike or a perceived inability to succeed) are equally telling. Almost all of these decisions have been based on your personal preferences and interests. Rarely are these choices random. The concept that underlies the myth of Ariadne's Thread is the ability you have to construct your own guide to your future, to discover a life's work that will be meaningful and fulfilling. We do find that the concept of following your own Thread can be helpful as you consider the choices that come your way, and those that you deliberately seek out and make happen.

From the Ariadne myth there developed a problem-solving methodology referred to as Ariadne's Thread. This is a process whereby the problem solver takes a possible route to a solution all the way to its logical conclusion, and, upon meeting a dead end, backtracks to the point at which the last successful decision was made. For example, one follows a "thread," which could be a pencil line on a paper maze or a record of numbers on a pad or a computer to help solve a Sudoku puzzle. Then the failed choice is recorded and the new "path" is followed to its conclusion. Ariadne's Thread is an inductive reasoning process that attempts to reach conclusions based on the pursuit of specific evidence.

We have long wanted to write a book that concentrates expressly on college undergraduates and recent graduates in their twenties and thirties regarding their planning for their future. Out of confusion, uncertainty, peer and parental pressures, or lack of sufficient research and planning, far too many post-collegians automatically consider the most visible, traditional careers. These fields are often overpopulated, and the competition for entry positions is keen. We refer to the pattern as default decision making for far too many educated individuals get stuck in this dead end.

The thought process goes something like this: "Since I don't know what I really want to accomplish with my life, or how to make carefully thought-out choices, I will opt for the field or graduate school that my parents, my friends, or the larger community values or tells me is right for me." These careers may be highly stressful and not necessarily fulfilling. The most typical of these choices are medicine, banking, finance, law, technology, marketing, and advertising. Rising numbers of college graduates enter the job market annually at a time when opportunities in these traditional fields are shrinking and the competition for meaningful employment among recent graduates is increasing exponentially. The economic downturn in 2008 and 2009 has made the choice of the right career path and graduate program even more important and difficult. Applications to law and business schools, traditional safe harbors during recessions, are increasing, though many applicants may not have considered whether these costly and competitive programs are truly appropriate for them. Entry-level opportunities at financial services, real estate, and other firms affected most dramatically by the economic crisis are diminishing, taking away many of the traditional first-job choices of college graduates.

As a result, a majority of individuals are turning to graduate schools, internships, or jobs they feel indifferently about as alternatives, often with little consideration of what their education or personal experience has prepared them for. Considering what they actually want to accomplish in their lifetime is little more than an afterthought. Many individuals who have already completed graduate degrees in specialized fields at great expense find themselves disappointed or disillusioned in their present circumstances. The average debt load for a significant portion of college undergraduates has doubled in the past decade to an average of more than $20,000. This makes the choice of a profession and the prospect of graduate school as a step toward these goals daunting and potentially unrealistic because of the rise in competitive applicants across the spectrum of programs. Add to that debt the additional loan burden of a law or medical degree, for example, and graduates can find their career choices even more restricted.

Of even greater concern in our counseling experience are those who choose career paths or graduate degrees because they feel obliged to, or without giving careful enough thought to how these choices fit with their personal strengths, interests, and passions. Far too many make decisions guided by familiarity, money, luck, family, or facility, and later come to regret, as Robert Frost put it, "The Road Not Taken." We want you to plan, as much as you can, a considered life.

This book is aimed at well-educated, predominantly liberal arts college students and graduates whose predicament have not been expressly addressed in the books out there on getting a job and finding a career. We focus on more imaginative thinking about the social, economic, technical, demographic, educational, and family- and work-style trends, and their implications for selecting a fulfilling career. We will cover some of the key patterns or concepts that such individuals typically encounter in their search. There is a proliferation of books on "how to get a job by writing the best résumé and selling yourself in the interview." These have little or no focus on educated young adults who are seeking direction in how to choose a professional career, or to discover their vocation or calling, which would enable them to utilize their educational skills, intellectual interests, and personal values and commitments that they have developed and honed over the course of their collegiate experience.

In our many interviews with college students and graduates, we listen to them talk about wanting to identify a calling rather than merely a job. The focus of this book will be on finding your calling, by which we mean a life's work that meets your emotional and intellectual needs. We will touch on a series of concepts that should ring true for you if you're caught in the maze of making major life-work decisions. We encourage you to begin with an exploration of your aptitudes, skills, talents, wants, and needs that can lead to a discovery of a host of careers that are ideal for you. We will provide you with recommendations regarding the most important questions you need to ask yourself and others in a position to assist you in your search.

Because many college graduates feel they lack specific technical or vocational training to compete in the job market, we highlight the major abilities that the liberal arts college graduate has developed through his or her education and the ways in which these skills transfer to meaningful careers. We have found that our discussion of these attributes in our Greenes' Guides series has had a positive impact on many student readers and their parents.

We have tapped into our personal relationships with leaders in a wide array of fields and asked them to discuss the nature of their work, the skill sets and personal traits required to excel and find fulfillment in their professions, and their personal life Threads. Their answers will surprise you and educate you about the decisions you must make and the factors you should consider. We also present case studies of young adults who found their calling after college through a thoughtful search process that reflects the steps we recommend. The range of personal histories and their outcomes will demonstrate for you the highly individualistic nature of choosing a career, the interesting career choices that frequently are overlooked, and the imaginative ways in which young adults can identify their goals and take the necessary steps to realize them.

INTRODUCTION

THE CHALLENGE OF
INVENTING YOUR OWN FUTURE

> The important thing in life is to have a great aim and to possess the aptitude and the perseverance to attain it.
>
> —JOHANN WOLFGANG VON GOETHE

"IF YOU DON'T LIKE WHAT you are doing, you are likely not to be very good at it." This observation on our part to many recent college graduates we have counseled is echoed by experienced leaders in the workplace, by professional career counselors, and what's most significant of all, by those who find themselves dissatisfied, unfulfilled, and depressed by their present employment and career choice. As increasing numbers of college educated young men and women ask for guidance on what they are best suited for, how they should plan for their future, and what they should do when they leave the relative security and structure of their college environment, their words and emotions add up to a desire to find their calling in life, whatever terminology they might use to identify their life's work. We encourage these voyagers to launch their own search by working back to the many Threads in their early lives: the myriad decisions they made along the way to get to where they are now. To reflect on what matters to them, what strikes a chord that resonates when considering the interests, activities, hobbies, people, settings, intellectual pursuits, games, and the college they have chosen up to this juncture in their lives. Almost always they discover a theme among these choices, which can become the metaphorical thread that leads them out of their sense of confusion and anxiety.

A majority of the thousands of college graduates we have counseled over the years have expressed their desire to find the right career, but most are concerned with how to go about this process in a complex, dynamic, and competitive environment. Most do not comprehend the distinction between a career and a vocation or calling. We find a clue lies in the classical derivation of the two terms: the word *career* comes from the Latin word *carrera,* which referred to a racetrack. Vocation is derived from the Latin *vocatio* or *vocare,* meaning "to call." Thus the word *vocation* is used today to refer to something deeper or more personal than a "job."

It seems clear that it is preferable to hear an inner voice beckoning you to an endeavor that feels worth doing, that provides an inner sense of well-being, that gives purpose to your life, while a career can mean a lifetime of going around in circles. When you choose your vocation you determine the lifestyle you wish to live and the legacy you desire to leave. The many research studies of workers—in all walks of life and levels of occupations through the years—consistently have found that what matters most in determining their satisfaction with their life is finding a meaning or value in their work; feeling that a sense of beauty that somehow is expressed by their efforts; having a sense of pride in what one does; and enjoying a respect from others as a result of their efforts. There is a natural instinct to desire a feeling of significance and a natural relationship with one's self-perception and work. We believe this is the impetus for your wanting to read this guide.

A calling should sustain you, nourish you, allow you to grow intellectually, emotionally, even spiritually, to call for increasing challenges and rewards as you use your natural talents and skills, and core beliefs. For all of us, finally identifying our calling is the result of a process of time, thought, experiences, and experimentation, rather than a purely rational choice or immediate knowledge. As Robert Frost said, "way leads on to way," each decision and event leads to another and another. You must consider this approach in order to find the destination that is at present a glimmer in your mind, or a half-realized desire.

As we discuss in chapter 2, you can succeed in any field of endeavor because of your educational background in the liberal arts. What are the most significant elements for success according to leaders in virtually all career fields? The following list of positive characteristics should resonate with your educational and personal experiences that have brought you to this point in your life as a college student or graduate:

- Communications skills, oral and written
- Teamwork capability
- Interpersonal aptitude
- Work ethic
- Sense of honesty and values
- Inherent motivation and initiative
- Analytical and problem solving
- Numerical ability
- Computer literacy
- Adaptability and resiliency
- Social and emotional maturity
- Research capability
- Perseverance

We often use the words *passion* and *passionate* when talking with students heading toward college, choosing a major concentration and extracurricular activities while in college, and then when beginning a plan to define their future goals and direction. None of you could have gotten this far in your life without having discovered and developed passions for some interest and activity. That passion has likely defined much of who you are, whom you associate with, what you look forward to on a regular basis, what keeps you up when you should be sleeping, or consumes time and energy when you could be studying for an exam or completing a paper.

During the 1970s, then the president of Dartmouth College, John Kemeny, told students that almost all of the careers that they were likely to spend their lives involved in had not yet been invented. This statement, from an educator who developed the computer language BASIC that facilitated the personal computer explosion, has proven prophetic. But even this eloquent spokesman for the virtues and advantages of a liberal arts education, who had advanced training both in mathematics and philosophy, could not have imagined fully the extraordinary developments in technology and global expansion that are affecting virtually all areas of our personal and professional lives. If experienced governmental and business leaders, economic and technical planners, and futurists continue to be challenged in predicting the next major issues and developments that will impact the national and international environment, how can a twenty-something-year-old be expected to plan with confidence for her future?

It was Mark Twain, never a fan of formal education, who quipped: "All you need in this life is ignorance and confidence, and then Success is sure." We doubt that this was a workable formula in Twain's time and it is certainly not the case today. The ancient Greeks, in their perception of the uncertainties of their environment, were fond of saying: "If you want to make the Gods laugh, tell them you have a plan." This is an observation that holds truer today than at any time in our recorded history. Here are but a few gems of misguided perceptions of what the future would hold: in 1899 the Chief of the United States Patent Office declared that "everything that can be invented has been invented." In 1943 Tom Watson, the founder and president of IBM said, "I think there is a world market for maybe five large computers." In 1981 Bill Gates is said to have proclaimed that, "640K ought to be enough for anyone." Casey Stengel, the legendary manager of the New York Yankees, was astute in his thought, if not his speech, when he told a reporter, "I never make predictions— at least not about the future."

The point of this scenario is self-evident: advances in science, technology, communications, global access and interaction, and knowledge of how and why we behave as we do are advancing at such an exponential rate that we cannot plan with authority or confidence every future step any of us will take. The younger we are, the more changes we will see over a lifetime. Your educational foundation, regardless of your field of study, will prove indispensable for doing essential reading, research, questioning, and interviewing with experts and practitioners. Together with your critical and honest self-evaluation, this will create the thread that will lead you from the dark zone of doubt and confusion to a direction that feels right for you.

We will emphasize further the importance of utilizing the skills and training you have accumulated through your formal education, as well as part-time jobs, volunteer efforts, and internships, to help you research the future as best you can. This is the start of using the virtual toolbox you have created and have been adding to since your earliest days. Now you will open it up and put to use the implements that lie within to carry out your search. One of the most powerful factors that affects our social, economic, and physical universe is the dynamic of human demographics. At any time in our history, the demographic composition of a particular society and its continual changes play a significant role in how we live and what challenges and choices we have. Let us bring this universal dynamic closer to home for you.

Many of the opportunities that await you will be determined by population trends. In fact they already have in a number of ways. The population explosion that occurred after World War II, creating the generation of baby boomers (your parents), resulted in an expansion in all sectors of our economy, together with the growth of educational programs and opportunities unimagined in any earlier time. Schools and colleges, graduate programs, and research facilities grew dramatically and resulted in the most educated population of any nation in the world. Research and innovations in science and technology, medicine, and inventions that served the public's insatiable appetite for more comfortable living led to the growth of new businesses, new ways of doing business, more leisure time for other endeavors, more women able to join the workforce, and more money to spend across the economy.

The impact on your lives of demographic factors is extraordinary in many ways. The number of places in education, particularly at the college level, has opened unlimited choices. The tools you use to work and play with are readily available and affordable. The range and number of careers are well beyond those available to your parents. Statistically you represent the down side of the high peak of the population in this country. Those boomers have aged and will soon become the largest senior population in history. Their interests and needs will affect the economics of the marketplace and opportunities for the generation they brought into this world. Here are some specific demographics predicted by the U.S. Department of Labor for 2016 to consider as you plan for your future calling:

- The U.S. population will continue to grow by 22 million. Minority groups will represent the largest portion of this growth.

- The biggest group of the population, 30 percent, will be the baby boomers who range in age from 55 to 64.

- The primary working force cohort, 24 to 55 years old, will decline from 68 percent to 64 percent of the population.

- The greatest expansion in careers will occur in the professions. The largest growth will be in education and health fields, followed by scientific, technical, mathematical, financial, managerial, and information and communications areas.

- There will be a significant growth in both private (nonprofit), governmental, and public service organizations to meet the needs of an expanding national and international population.

- The prediction is that 7 million new jobs in the professions will need to be added to the workplace.

Why bring in these data here? To make the point that the future needs of our society will be ever more dependent on a population of young, well-educated individuals. The opportunities are out there; the challenge is to determine for yourself which direction appeals the most for the right reasons.

Here is Tricia's story. While still on her path of discovery she has accomplished a great deal already by following her instincts and her interests without worrying obsessively where they would eventually lead her. Like so many liberal arts graduates, Tricia majored in the humanities, in this case, English Literature. Her writing and communication skill sets have served her well as she has pursued her goals. We asked her: What is the Thread that you have followed during your life, that has helped you find your way? What mattered to you most as you made the important decisions about your life's direction?

FROM THE TIME THAT I was a child, I had always been fascinated by other cultures and languages. It is certainly not the norm for a black woman of Caribbean descent from Brooklyn to become a dyed in the wool Russophile! I still have vague memories of myself as a five-year-old begging my mother to buy me a book called *See It and Say It in German*.

Upon graduating from college, I discovered several training schools that offered TEFL (Teaching English as a Foreign Language), all of which were located in San Francisco. I have to admit that being an educator was not the priority. To my surprise, I did very well in the program, graduating first in my class. I was planning to go abroad to teach, when I got into a horrible car accident, which left me injured for a while and, unfortunately, I had to give up my teaching plans. I thought the dream was dead.

I returned to New York City to convalesce and reevaluate. Once my injury had healed, I got a job at the College Board, the organization best known for the creation of the SAT examination. My education experience opened the door to working for this mysterious and well-respected organization. In a few short years, I moved up to Associate Director of School-Level Services. I traveled extensively all over the United States, organizing trainings and managing national exams. It was a lot of responsibility for someone so young, but I felt up to the task.

However, something was still missing and I couldn't put my finger on it, but I was about to find out. One of the benefits of working at the College Board was tuition reimbursement for non-degree-bearing programs. I decided, since one of the College Board examinations that I was managing was a Spanish exam, that I would learn Spanish—in Spain.

When I arrived in Spain, I had the opportunity to work with a side project that the language school was doing with students in Morocco. I knew at once that this was the aspect of education that I needed to be in. But how would I get there? Slowly, it dawned on me, that I should look into international education graduate programs, even though many of my colleagues thought that a domestically focused education degree would be more useful professionally. I applied to the master's program in International Education Development at Columbia University. My thinking was this field would be a perfect confluence of my love for education and the exploration of other cultures.

I completed my master's degree and am now a Ph.D. student in Comparative and International Education at Columbia. I worked throughout my master's program at the Ford Foundation International Fellowships Programs. This is a $350 million program that provides graduate education opportunities for marginalized people for 22 developing countries in Africa, Asia, Latin America, the Middle East, and Russia. I have had the opportunity to consult on a number of interesting projects aimed at improving education both domestically and internationally.

Though it has not been a straight line, I feel that because I never lost sight of my goal of international work, I am now in the best position that I have ever been to make it a reality.

In response to our asking what advice she would give to college students and young adults as they seek their calling and attempt to build their careers accordingly, Tricia offered an overview.

> I WOULD ENCOURAGE YOUNG COLLEGE-EDUCATED men and women to try many different things before committing to something that will become their "career." I was told early in my work that international education would not lead anywhere; yet I am living proof that it has led me everywhere. It is important to keep looking at opportunities as each experience builds on the others and leads to the next experience that fits with your dreams. Also, find yourself a mentor, an experienced and wise person who appreciates what you are looking for and is willing to guide you and be responsive to your questions.

The present environment foretells a competitive marketplace for emerging college graduates. There has been a continuous rise in the number of college graduates and greater competition for the right careers and for graduate education. In 2008 there were 18 million students enrolled full time in our colleges and universities. In 2009 1.6 million of them graduated and either entered the job market or graduate school. Talk about demographic forces at work! Of those 1.6 million graduates, 954,000 were women (NCES, USDE).

Each succeeding year, more women enroll in our colleges and go on to graduate. In the past decade the increase in female graduates was 33 percent—a statistic that has great significance for our private and public institutions and professions. The growing gap in the ratio of female to male graduates and the impact on career choices and opportunities will necessitate adjustments in virtually all career and vocational endeavors. As more educated women as well as racial and ethnic minorities of both sexes, assume more professional and leadership roles, adjustments will have to be made to accommodate their needs and interests. Business as usual will not be an acceptable mode of operation in all professions. Already more women than men are enrolled in master's and doctoral degree programs, and men and women are enrolled in equal numbers in law and medical schools. Only engineering, technology, and business programs enroll higher proportions of men.

Our goal and our hope for you is that you will allow yourself to imagine what the next phase of your life will be—and to consider one that satisfies and fulfills your desires and needs—so that you can invent your own future. A theme that we repeat intentionally throughout this guide is that your education has prepared you to contend with the challenge of finding your way in such a complicated, contentious, and competitive society. You will need to strengthen some of those skills that you have used in making your way through your earlier life and especially your college years. These include:

- Agility to adapt to new and different groups of people with whom you have lived and from whom you have learned;

- The ability to embrace new ideas and concepts that are often at odds with earlier suppositions learned at home and school;

- The capacity to analyze, organize, and synthesize mountains of information, theories, and data;

- A heightened curiosity to keep abreast of new concepts and trends in the worlds of science, technology, commerce, medicine, and international affairs through constant reading and discussion with knowledgeable individuals;

- The skill to be able to put your thoughts together in a clear and coherent fashion orally and in print; and

- The capacity to cope with the demands placed on you by your teachers, coaches, activity directors, and the resulting stress.

The talented futurist thinker and writer, Alvin Toffler, put it this way after predicting the major changes and challenges that lay ahead for the individual and the state: "The illiterate of the 21st Century will not be those who cannot read and write, but those who cannot learn, unlearn, and relearn." You, the reader of this guide, are blessed to have the ability to read and write, as well as having your past educational experiences of learning and relearning that you will continually build on throughout your life. You are equipped with the tools to move forward to find your vocation and use it to discover a lifetime that works for you and for the larger community of which you are a part.

You will read throughout this guide the personal stories of successful and fulfilled individuals who found their calling by means of the process we recommend you follow. While these individuals represent a wide variety of career choices, they share the experience of having found the way to their present vocation by studying the various Threads of their earlier lives which developed over time into a coherent picture of what they wanted, or rather what they *needed* to do with their lives. They were eager to share their stories of how they found their way out of the labyrinth to their calling.

In the following chapters we will cover a range of key concepts for you to consider as you look for clues and follow your Threads through the labyrinth in which you currently find yourself. We hope that by the end of this book, you not only have some clear directions to pursue, but also some sense of what will matter most as you make essential decisions.

1

IDENTIFYING THE THREADS THAT TIE YOUR LIFE TOGETHER

> Nothing is so difficult but that it may be found out by seeking.
>
> —TERENCE, *HEAUTON TIMORUMENOS*

WHO ARE YOU? THE PROCESS of planning for a career, pursuing your education, discovering a vocation or calling, and looking for a job should take place over period of time and involve extensive and intensive self-evaluation and reflection. That is how you will find the Thread or Threads that connect your life's path.

Some of you might be sitting on the couch hoping that some type of a lightbulb, perhaps a compact fluorescent these days, will flash on above your head with the perfect idea. Maybe a random TV commercial or e-mail from a friend will trigger your *aha!* moment. "Man," you'll say, "I should be a pilot. I've always liked to travel!"

You'll take a long shower. You've always thought better in the shower. "That's it!" you'll cry. "Anthropology!"

If you're hoping for this kind of revelatory experience, you're likely going to wait a long time to be awakened from your stupor. Even worse, you might find yourself jumping into a new career or enrolling in a graduate program, without thinking your decision through. The likelihood of your remaining in your newfound "perfect job for me" seems low. At least, the odds of your remaining happy there don't seem high.

LEADING A CONSIDERED LIFE

Believe it or not, you are not the first person in history to confront the dilemma of deciding what you should do with your life. How should you live it? What is important to you? These questions have occupied humanity for millennia. Socrates argued that "the unconsidered life is not worth living." But you do not need to be a philosopher to aspire to living a considered life, in which you make conscious choices about your values, lifestyle, friendships, environment, and work. Particularly today, we live in a society where you have the freedom to be or become almost anything or anyone you can imagine. If you have a college education, then you are even better positioned to take advantage of the many opportunities for self-definition and advancement, as well as community service and development.

Are there constraints? To be sure. Little is earned without effort and sacrifice. You might never reach some goals (becoming the President of the United States, flying the Space Shuttle, starring in a Hollywood blockbuster, or winning a Nobel Prize come to mind), but along the way you will likely accomplish much of what you seek. We believe that this is particularly true if you have thought carefully about your skills, strengths, values, and goals, and then crafted and pursued a life plan.

Much of what we discuss in this book focuses on getting you to consider your life. Too many of you will have gotten to this point in your life without questioning yourselves. Perhaps you have followed the advice, subtle or otherwise, of your parents or other family members. Maybe you did what you thought you were supposed to do, or what your community's values suggested was "what people did." We have found many college students and graduates declaring that, past getting into and graduating from college, they hadn't really thought about what came next. In one instance, we recall a young woman working on a stock trading floor who was miserable in her job.

"When I graduated college," she lamented, "I was told I had three options: law, medicine, and business. Since I didn't like reading all that much, and didn't like science, I figured business was the way to go." Even within this narrow band of choices, she happened into a first job with an aggressive, male-oriented stock trading company. She found not only the substance of the work unpleasant, but her coworkers rude, competitive, and openly hostile. Had she considered her preferences for the kind of work and work environment that would likely be more appropriate for her, she might have launched her career more wisely.

IDENTIFYING YOUR THREADS

Where and how should you start to consider your life and your life's work? We have been using the metaphor of a thread for some time now to help students and graduates begin to trace their key motivations and interests. We have asked many professionals from a variety of fields to look back on their life and draw the same kinds of connections. Everyone has a Thread or Threads to follow.

Is there a Thread that has connected what you have done and what you have enjoyed throughout your life to date? What have you been passionate about, proficient in, or rewarded for? Where do you feel most at home? There are some classic career Threads you might be familiar with. The architect who always enjoyed playing with Lego blocks. The chemist who as a child always spent time concocting potions in the kitchen. The lawyer who, as a small fry, argued and negotiated, more or less successfully, with his or her parents. Perhaps your Thread turns out to be similarly self-evident. We suspect, however, that since you are reading this book, it probably isn't so obvious.

We believe that, in most instances, our Threads emerge over time, often intertwining, disappearing, and reemerging in the course of our development and exposure to new ideas, people, and environments. Consider the following thoughtful response to our Thread question from a senior corporate executive, Erv Shames, who has served as CEO or president of such companies as Kraft Foods, General Foods, Borden, and Stride Rite, and who now devotes significant time to volunteer work and teaching business courses at the Darden School of the University of Virginia.

THE CASE OF ERV SHAMES

I have always been a goal-oriented person who has a need to understand where I am trying to go and how I should try to get there, so early on, I came to several conclusions relevant to my path in life.

1. I wanted to achieve a position of leadership and influence at as senior a level as my capabilities could provide.

2. My best chance of success would come from under-standing my skills and finding a career where those skills were critical to success.

I have identified five Threads that ran through my career de-cisions:

1. **Interest in understanding people, especially what motivates and interests them.** I grew up in a tiny farm town in Iowa where my parents owned and worked in a small retail business. My brother and I were involved in the business from an early age. I was fascinated with figuring out what consumers might want to buy and how to sell it to them.

2. **Enjoyment of working with a group for a common purpose.** I had the opportunity of serving in leader-ship positions in organizations in high school and college. I found that I seemed to have a skill in bring-ing people together to define what we wanted to ac-complish and then in motivating them to get it done.

3. **Desire to achieve financial success and security.** My parents ran into financial difficulties while I was in college. I saw the negative impacts that this had on their life. This drove me to want to acquire enough fi-nancial wherewithal to have financial security and to have the freedom to try different careers if I so chose. I

remember, in the latter, being advised that "life is not a dress rehearsal. There are no second acts."

4. **Desire to contribute to society, to make a difference.** I am not sure of the genesis of this, but it might have been because both of my parents were involved in community service as presidents of service organizations, charities, and the local school board. It might also have stemmed from growing up in the South in the late 1950s and early '60s and seeing up close the social injustices of segregation.

5. **Desire to be a good husband and father.** I did not want to choose a career, which would stand in the way of my being physically and mentally available to my family. This could happen by choosing a job in which the time and travel demands made me physically unavailable, or choosing a job where my struggle to perform well made me mentally unavailable. I needed to choose a career where I could succeed on "my terms."

A major challenge for me was to reconcile my desire to succeed in business with my desire to contribute to society. In thinking about societal impact, the objective—the top of the giving-back pyramid—was to be able to have a positive influence on the lives of a large number of people. Because of my involvement in my family's business, I initially enrolled as a business major in college. I became dissatisfied with the narrowness of this choice so I switched in my sophomore year to a major that allowed me to take as many liberal arts courses as possible while still graduating in four years.

After graduating from college, I worked for two years and then decided to get a graduate degree. I debated between law school and business school. I decided that business school was a better match with my skills. At business school, marketing courses were the ones I was most attracted to and the most successful in. During the job interview process in my second year at business school, I found that consumer goods companies were the ones that most valued marketing skills and where brand management skills had the best chance of leading to a top management position.

When I got into my career, there were many lucky breaks that enabled me to advance quickly. I was also, with the support of my company, able to find ways to contribute to others along the way. For instance, after I had been with the company only two years, I started Operation Opportunity along with two of my coworkers. This is a program that provides summer jobs to high school students in Westchester County and company mentors, and for every dollar the students earn during the summer another dollar is placed in escrow for their further education. This program is now in its fortieth year of operation and has helped thousands of students.

When I became CEO of various companies, we instituted programs within the companies that threw open the door for hiring and advancing all employees regardless of background. We also used our corporate clout to encourage our employees to be involved outside the company and supported community organizations that furthered the values of the company. Frankly, it is easy to become a "community leader" when you have the resources of a significant corporation to back you up.

My family life has been wonderful; I've had a strong marriage, two great children, and now four terrific grandchildren. A lot of this successful family outcome is due to my wife and my children. Some part though is due to making career choices that helped me be available.

After 30 years in business with the last 10 in CEO-type positions, I decided to retire from active management and pursue another path. I characterize that path as a portfolio career, comprised one-third of nonprofit board involvement, one-third for-profit board involvement and one-third in a new learning experience, which for me turned out to be teaching.

My path has been based on sorting out what my skills were and what mattered to me, both financially and nonfinancially, and then identifying industries and companies where those skills are highly valued and my interests could be met. By doing this I believe that my odds of success and satisfaction were significantly enhanced.

Erv presents a wonderful example on several fronts. Note that he switched his major out of business in college and was still able to move to a graduate degree in business and a very successful business career. By carefully considering how and where he could make a difference and satisfy the various needs he consciously identified over time, Erv was able to do well and do good, using his excellence in marketing and consumer brands as a base from which to change company practices, promote community involvement, and improve the lives of employees. He now uses his areas of expertise on both for-profit and nonprofit boards and to give back through his teaching of future business leaders. We hope that you'll see how Erv was able to integrate the Threads of his life in ways that helped him be successful, as well as satisfied with what he has been able to accomplish for himself and for others.

To identify your Threads, and know which to follow and how, you can do something as simple as a listing of priorities, strengths, and interests to get yourself thinking more consciously about who you are and what you want to do with your life. That can give you a framework within which you can consider job and career options. You can also find a number of resources to help you structure your thinking, and discover and organize your Threads. These include books and articles; printed evaluation forms and programs, such as the Myers-Briggs Type Indicator (MBTI) and Johnson O'Connor aptitude testing; online self-evaluation instruments like Monster's Job Assets and Strengths Profiler (JASPER); and one-on-one work with career and graduate school counselors.

UTILIZING SELF-ASSESSMENT TOOLS

Self-assessment is an ongoing process, one that you have likely begun already during high school and college. This might have included formal evaluation instruments, or work with a teacher, guidance counselor, or adviser to begin considering your strengths, skills, and interests. You might have talked with family, friends, and mentors in an academic or employment setting.

First and foremost, a more directed, formal self-assessment will involve reading, and lots of it. We encourage you to take on a conscious program of learning about various career fields, job search resources, and personal analytical tools. Here is a list of just some of the many good resources available to you.

CAREER PLANNING AND
SELF-ASSESSMENT RESOURCES

Assessment.com
www.assessment.com
Source for the Motivational Appraisal of Personal Potential (MAPP) and other assessments.

CareerBuilder.com
www.careerbuilder.com
Assessment tools and job search tools, particularly helpful for those seeking
business careers or considering business degrees.

Chronicle of Higher Education
www.chronicle.com/jobs/tools
Resources for those interested in careers in academia, as well as extensive
data on colleges, universities, and trends in education.

College Board
www.myroad.collegeboard.com
College major and career planning from your friends who brought you
the SAT.

CPP, Inc.
www.cpp.com
Source for the MBTI, Strong Interest Inventory, Thomas-Kilmann Conflict
Mode, and other evaluation instruments.

Experience
www.experience.com
A site for college graduates and young professionals offering career planning
tips and resources.

Jobweb
www.jobweb.com
Career planning and job search for college students and graduates.

Johnson O'Connor Research Foundation
www.jocrf.org
An on-site testing program to help you assess your aptitudes (natural skills and abilities).

Monster
www.monster.com
A job search and career development site, which also features articles on career planning and the JASPER self-assessment tool.

NACElink Network
www.nacelink.com
A resource available through college career services offices that allows you to search job postings and access career planning materials. See if your college is involved.

Naviance
www.naviance.com/products/workspacek12/cp
Many high schools use the Naviance suite of college planning and application services, which also includes career planning tools for students. If your high school uses Naviance, you can complete a Career Interest Profile and search for careers by their Holland interest codes.

One Day, One Job
www.onedayonejob.com
An interesting site offering tips and connections for recent college graduates hoping to find the right entry-level job.

O*Net Online
www.online.onetcenter.org
An extensive list of occupations and worker characteristics. Also offers a Skills Search self-assessment.

U.S. Bureau of Labor Statistics
www.bls.gov/oco/cg
Source for the *Career Guide to Industries and the Occupational Outlook Handbook,* providing information on jobs and employment trends.

WetFeet
www.wetfeet.com
Career planning and job seeking resources.

Assessment tools tend to cluster into several distinct types. The first seeks to measure and organize your thinking around *personality types.* Instruments like the MBTI help you understand your preferences for the ways in which you interact with other people; the environments in which you like to work; the ways in which you process information and learn; and generally how you view the world. Once you have identified your "type," your task is then to match this type with one or more career fields in which people with similar personality types have thrived. The Strong Interest Inventory, for example, can be matched with the MBTI to connect particular jobs to your personality type.

You will often hear people who have been through the MBTI process, or who work in an office environment that utilizes the instrument regularly, discuss their type and ask, "So, what are you?" For example, someone might note they are an ENTJ. Huh? The Myers-Briggs system defines four elements associated with personality and differentiates between types according to these four aspects. They are Extroversion versus Introversion; Sensing versus iNtuition; Thinking versus Feeling; and Judging versus Perceiving. We have found that the MBTI evaluation can help organize the way you think about yourself, and give you a sense of your *tendencies*. You are likely to exhibit a combination of the Myers-Briggs types, but in some cases you might see a very strong preference toward, for example, Thinking (concentrating on logic and reason-based decisions) versus Feeling (emphasizing values and concern for others in your choices). As a tool to help you begin to understand yourself, how you like to work, and where and how you tend to be most comfortable, the MBTI can open up discussions of new careers, as well as different roles within your current career environment.

The second type of assessment tool looks at your natural aptitudes and abilities: What are you good at? The Johnson O'Connor Research Foundation's approach is to assess fixed aptitudes, such as a facility working with numbers, communicating with people verbally, or working with visual artistic media. These are seen as distinct from interests, which can change over time, and more connected to specific career choices. Again, this kind of testing can be a wonderful tool for you to measure your strengths against a larger population and to see which career paths would match well with what you are good at. Now, presumably you tend to like and succeed in that which comes naturally to you, so unlocking a natural aptitude and making the connection to a job that would allow you to utilize that skill can prove a real accomplishment. We would note that your aptitudes are also likely to connect to your Thread or Threads, which we presented earlier.

Another example of making connections between skills and careers is offered by the Occupational Information Network. Whether you have found out about some of your skills or aptitudes through personal reflection, talking with others, reading job or teacher evaluations of your work, or going through some testing like the Johnson O'Connor program, you can input your skills into an online assessment at O*Net OnLine and find any number of jobs that match your profile. Again, this is a starting point. The same profile of skills could produce a match with firefighting, clinical psychology, art, and athletic training. You're going to need to do some additional work to figure out which of these jobs represents your dream career.

EXPLORING COLLEGE CAREER SERVICES OFFICES

Have you ever visited, spoken with, or looked at the Web site of your college's Career Services Office? Why aren't we surprised if your answer is "no," "huh?," or "oh, there was one?" In our discussions with current college students and graduates we find that in most cases students have never set foot in the office of their career and graduate school planning office. Most students don't seem to know such a resource exists, even as many tend to complain about the lack of good counseling and mentoring at their college.

These days, career offices are not "placement" services that match students with employers. Rather, these offices are there to facilitate your exploration of your interests and your planning. According to Kathy Sims, director of the career center at UCLA, "We teach [students] how to make effective and thoughtful and deliberate decisions" (*Chronicle of Higher Education*). Paradoxically, as desperate as most of you are for career help and advising, most of you do your best to avoid taking advantage of this major resource available to you during and after you graduate college. Are all college offices excellent in terms of their staff, knowledge base, facilities, and contacts? Of course not. But there are many good offices and counselors out there who can serve as coaches, allies, and sounding boards for you.

Career services offices play many roles today. They facilitate graduate school planning, for example, by coordinating with a college's premedical advising program, the registrar (who is responsible for sending official transcripts), and the faculty (who write your recommendation letters, which may be kept on file at the office). Career offices typically maintain an alumni networking database to help you search for jobs and internships with graduates working in your fields of interest. They may coordinate this function with your college's alumni relations office. Career counselors host corporate, military, public service, and nonprofit recruiting fairs and individual visits. Many counselors actively promote your college's name and programs to attract potential recruiters to campus. Counselors can also help facilitate applications for competitive grants and fellowships, such as the Marshall, Fulbright, Rhodes, and Udall scholarships.

Some career services offices maintain extensive Web sites with the college's own self-evaluation and career matching tools. For example, Vanderbilt offers an Individualized Coaching Action Plan (ICAP) that students complete prior to their first visit to the office. The survey helps students consider initial career interests and what they have accomplished to date, which they then discuss with a career counselor at the office. According to Jim Bellar, Senior Assistant Director of the Career Center, "Activities are written on the ICAP as action plan steps. The coach also makes a copy of the plan for the student, and it is recorded in case note" (*Campus Career Counselor* newsletter). Following such initial visits, you can find many workshops at college career centers, focusing on, for example, mock interviews, résumé and cover-letter writing, self-assessment, and employment trends and opportunities.

Some Web site materials might be limited to a college's own students and graduates, while in other cases, colleges

A SAMPLING OF COLLEGE CAREER SERVICES WEB SITES

University of Arizona
www.career.arizona.edu

Dartmouth College
www.dartmouth.edu/~csrc

Lawrence University
www.lawrence.edu/dept/student_dean/career

Lehigh University
www.lehigh.edu/careerservices

Princeton University
www.web.princeton.edu/sites/career

Vanderbilt University
www.vanderbilt.edu/career

University of Washington
www.careers.washington.edu

Washington University in St. Louis
www.careers.wustl.edu

make their information available to the wider public. Some offices also offer blogs with tips, trends, links, and strategies. Here are some examples of great career services Web sites we have found at a variety of colleges. Make sure to visit yours.

NEXT STEPS

As you continue your self-evaluation, you will want to consider what you know—about yourself, and about the world. Later in the book, we will discuss the concepts of a calling, a vocation, an avocation, a job, and a career, at more length. For now, we encourage you to begin considering what you have learned as a college student, and how your education has informed your sense of yourself; your skills and interests; and your Threads. Are you beginning to see aptitudes that have emerged more forcefully during or after college? Is there a Thread that you have followed during college that has guided your course selection, choice of major, choice of adviser, and participation in activities?

2

THE LIBERAL ARTIST GOES TO WORK

ALL TOO FREQUENTLY WE HEAR liberal arts college students at some critical point state in a plaintive tone, "I love my undergraduate concentration, but what good is it going to do me in getting a job and making a living? Wouldn't I be better off if I majored in a practical field like business or technology or computer science? Should I have bypassed a liberal arts college for a high-level vocational education?" And if it is not you, the student, who voices this concern, very often it is your parents who do. However, even if you majored in a more "practical" discipline like business, math, or engineering, you still might be feeling a disconnect between your educational program and the requirements of the Real World.

We are firm believers in the value of a liberal arts college education, as are employers across many career fields. Following your Thread through a liberal arts college will not only prepare you for the rest of your life, but also help you identify your strengths and interests along the way. Here are some of the qualities you are likely to have developed during your college years which will make you a better person *and* help you succeed in whatever career you select.

PERSONAL OUTCOMES OF A LIBERAL ARTS EDUCATION

Let's review the essential qualities that should emerge from a challenging undergraduate education and compare them to those that are essential for success in virtually all fields of professional endeavor. In the Introduction, we mentioned some of the important elements for career success mentioned by leaders in many fields. Here are some Key Habits of Mind, which are skills you likely developed in the course of your college education. They match up quite nicely with the skills employers are seeking. Key Habits of Mind include:

- **Critical analysis** of data, information, opinions, and events for their relevance, credibility, and objectivity;

- **Problem solving** that requires the application of multiple strategies and methodologies to complex situations or choices;

- **Reasoning ability** that calls for constructing an idea, a point of view, or a theory, and for interpreting complex issues or concepts and theories or ideas put forth by others;

- **Intellectual curiosity** that reflects a genuine interest in exploring new ideas and fields of study;

- **Developed writing and oral skills** that enable you to express your own ideas, as well as to interpret and analyze factual information and ideas provided by others in a clear, coherent, organized manner with a mature level of language usage;

- **Research capability** to locate relevant data and materials that will inform your studies and allow you to synthesize important information to be incorporated into your work; and,

- **Time management and study skills** that enable you to complete all of the academic demands of reading, writing, researching, and preparing for exams in an efficient and coherent manner.

Put these academic skills together with those personal qualities inherent in a successful college experience—all of which are sought after by employers—and you should feel equipped to take on any career that contains the sense of a personal calling. You have quite an elaborate tool kit in hand to deal with the challenges of a complex society and to take advantage of the countless opportunities that await you upon leaving college. The combination of an intellectual skill set, the habits of mind, and the social and emotional intelligence you developed through your college experience will allow you to plan your future as you would like it to be. Will this be an easy task, even taking into account your capabilities and desires? Of course not. But if you work through the Threads of your early life and can see the patterns that reflect your talents and interests, you will have a path to follow.

The creator of the Harry Potter series, J. K. Rowling, has a personal story as fascinating and inspirational as that of any of her fictional characters. In her commencement address at Harvard University in 2008, she recounted the difficult and painful path she traveled to attain her present extraordinary success. Talk about remaining true to one's earlier passion for writing and studying, in her case the classics, in the face of severe personal obstacles! Rowling's themes are the benefits of failure and the critical importance of imagination. Returning to her true love, classical literature and storytelling, she was, in time, able to fulfill what she calls her "big idea."

Often as we speak about the value both to the individual and society that is inherent in a liberal arts education, we get a reaction that indicates a lack of understanding of what constitutes a liberal arts curriculum. To many students it connotes an emphasis on the arts rather than the sciences. But actually, the beauty of a liberal arts curriculum is the exposure students get to a *broad* range of subjects, which helps us to interpret the world through the prism of such disciplines as the social sciences of political science, economics, psychology, and sociology; the visual and performing arts; the sciences of biology, chemistry, physics, and the environment; the humanities of literature, philosophy, history, and languages; and mathematics. Many of these subjects will, in time, become an essential background for your personal behavior and attitudes as well as the contributions you will make to your career.

As, if not more important are the personal values and beliefs that cannot help but be forged through the exposure to the varied social and philosophical ideas and ideals, the interpretations and critiques of our historical and legal past, the scientific principles and theories presented to you by your teachers, and your interactions with your fellow students. Every person we interviewed for this book stated outright that you cannot separate career goals from your value system and still expect to end up comfortable or fulfilled in your lifetime.

USING YOUR HEAD AND HEART TO KNOW YOURSELF BETTER

In their golden age of a democratic state, the ancient Greeks lived their lives by an ideal inscribed on the Temple of Apollo at Delphi, home of the Delphic Oracle, in two simple words: "Know Thyself." To know or understand oneself is seen as the basis for awareness and understanding not only of oneself, but of others and their actions and beliefs. Knowing what you value in your life is a constant exercise, possibly never completely fulfilled. From religious beliefs to moral standards, expectations of behavior to essential needs at the deepest emotional and spiritual levels, knowing yourself will help you make key choices in your life. Not working continuously on knowing the most about yourself—what truly matters to you on every level of your being—means that you will be less likely to find your way out of the labyrinth and on to the meaningful and rewarding role you should play in your adult life.

What you keep hearing is that you need to use both your head and your heart (okay, the gut is located somewhere below the heart, but you get the idea) to make important life decisions. You can and should learn from both success and failure, as we will discuss further on. Your liberal arts education will help you use all your intelligences—your cognitive and academic skills as well as emotional, creative, and interpersonal aptitudes—to assess the challenges and opportunities in your life and follow the right Thread.

Here is a major example of how your education and exercise in reading, researching, and talking with others can help you to find your direction: the leadership role Jeffrey Immelt, the chairman and CEO of General Electric Corporation, has assumed in the critical area of our global environment. Immelt is a corporate business leader with an engineering education at Dartmouth College, which included liberal courses in the social sciences. He is currently trustee of the college. He told an interviewer in the *Dartmouth Alumni Magazine,* "I get paid to see what's next. If I believe environmental evolution is what is next, I'm going to invest in that." Immelt coined the term *eco-imagination* to refer to the need for the business community to study the problems of global warming, greenhouse gas emission, and the conservation of earth's natural resources and to find solutions. He calls it a strategic policy of pro-business, pro-technology, and pro-conservation. Immelt has encouraged his alma mater to make sure that liberal arts colleges embrace the study of relevant sciences to meet "the convergence between health care, environmental science, chemistry, biology, and public policy." Consider the opportunities for you if you care about our planet, about the people who live on it, and the need to take care of those who require proper health care. A calling in any of these critical fields can be attained by exposure to a range of science and social science courses at the undergraduate level.

TAKING ADVANTAGE OF THE MANY JOB OPPORTUNITIES FOR COLLEGE GRADUATES

According to the Employment Policy Foundation, in the year 2000, when the U.S. economy was in an economic slump, 1.9

million Americans who had completed only high school were laid off. At the same time 1.2 million men and women with a college degree or vocational diploma were hired.

Those with a graduate-level degree, especially in the professional fields of law, business, education, and engineering, were virtually all employed in their field. Since the end of World War II, in any cycle of a stalled economy or recession, applications to professional graduate schools increased dramatically. It is a given that one of the many advantages liberal arts college graduates possess is the agility to undertake

ENGINEERS "THINKING OUTSIDE THE BOX"

Many engineering students and graduates are seeking work outside of traditional engineering-related fields today. According to Mary Sansalone, Dean of the School of Engineering at Washington University in St. Louis: "Today's engineering student is the innovative thinker, the student with the entrepreneurial bent, the student with the leadership and people skills, the student who wants to pursue the study of language and an international experience." More than 40 percent of Wash U's engineering students major in biomedical engineering, and go forward to work in fields that have "an impact on society." Others focus on sustainability issues at the university's Department of Energy, Environmental, and Chemical Engineering.

[Source: *Counselor's Canvas*, Washington University in St. Louis.]

advanced education as and when it seems appropriate to their professional advancement or calling.

We observed earlier the powerful role demographics play in education and employment, and here is how present trends play out for this generation of college graduates. The baby boom generation is now referred to regularly as the "graying generation"; some 76 million boomers will be retiring in the next couple of decades. This will create millions of job openings that will need to be filled. As we are well on our way to becoming a knowledge-based economy dealing in a globally competitive environment, an educated workforce of leaders, managers, and professional experts will become ever more critical. A period of limitless opportunities awaits you. Consider the demand for experts in the expanding fields of health and medicine; engineering and technology; business leadership for new enterprises as well as well-established corporations; government management; national and international politics; public, not-for-profit, and nongovernmental organizations; educational institutions at all levels; and the arts and entertainment. As old-fashioned as it may sound, the world is your oyster because of your liberal arts foundation, which for many includes concentrations in some of the fields mentioned here.

How frequently we hear the mantra of the contemporary universe of communications and media enterprises: content is king. We have experienced the import of this in our work as educators and writers. Our knowledge base has enabled us to write a goodly number of books and articles, to produce several national television specials for the Public Broadcasting Service, and to present seminars across the country. The more furious the expansion of the Internet and cable outlets, the greater the need for quality ideas, content, and presentation. It surely comes as no surprise that liberal arts graduates—with their broad knowledge base and sophisticated communications skills—are supplying so much of the creative content in today's multimedia landscape.

Here is some valuable input from a highly successful writer whose broad-based education helped to develop the skill sets he has used throughout his career. Tom Shachtman is an author, filmmaker, and educator who likes to joke that he has been gainfully unemployed for many years. This is

JOB OPPORTUNITIES EXPAND, BUT NOT NECESSARILY WHERE EXPECTED

According to the National Association of Colleges and Employers (NACE), the approximately 1.5 million college graduates of 2008 faced an uncertain job market, and one that did not grow as strongly as that for the previous college class. The finance and construction industries saw some of the most significant declines in job openings (7.5 percent and 2.8 percent, respectively). However, the utility industry reported a 49 percent increase, and the government sector a 32 percent growth in openings.

[Source: Tom A. Peter, *The Christian Science Monitor*, May 5, 2008, p.16.]

because he loves what he does for a living. And what he has accomplished is mightily impressive. He has written or coauthored 30 books, as well as magazine articles, a newspaper column, and visual documentaries. He has also taught at several major universities. A graduate of Tufts University with a degree in psychology, he earned an MFA degree from Carnegie Mellon University in playwriting. Like all those who have found their calling and been successful, Tom's early years provided a vital training ground for his present endeavors. Here are some of his observations and recommendations that he feels might prove helpful to more recent college graduates:

FOR A DECADE, I WORKED as a documentary filmmaker, training under the top men in the field at CBS News in the late 1960s, then going out on my own as writer-producer-director for the networks and local stations. Dealing with a variety of subjects, learning that there is always more than one way to get a point across, and seeking the input of others on one's creative projects are lessons that I have tried to carry over into writing books.

A *New York Times* review of a book of mine said that it was written "with passion and clarity," and if I have a goal, it is that this epithet could be said of all that I write and do in my life outside of my writing. Writers of nonfiction, like me, follow their curiosity wherever it takes them, and I have followed mine on a variety of interesting intellectual excursions, ranging broadly rather than specializing.

Here is the advice I would give to college students and young adults as they seek their calling and build their careers: Do what you like to do, and create your own yardsticks for evaluating your performance in these endeavors. Don't rely on others' yardsticks. But try to balance "doing your own thing" with the need to make a living, to maintain a roof over your head and that of your family. These need not be incompatible.

BECOMING WHOEVER YOU WANT TO BE AND DOING WHATEVER YOU CAN IMAGINE

Amy Lee Domini has used her ability to combine a liberal arts foundation with a strong set of personal values to become a force for good in the community. She is considered to be a leading voice for socially responsible investing. *Time* magazine named her to the Time 100 list of the world's most influential people in 2005. President Clinton honored her at a meeting of the Clinton Global Initiative, which was designed to protect children and the environment through the Domini Fund for International Giving.

In a recent ceremony at Berkeley Divinity School at Yale, Amy was awarded an honorary degree for her social service work. The citation noted that: "Earning a BA from Boston University in International and Comparative Studies with a stress on European History and Economics, you volunteered your time teaching adult education classes on the ABCs of investing, emphasizing its ethical and moral implications. Your first book, *Ethical Investing*, was the result of your conviction that socially responsible investing can not only contribute to human betterment but also make money." Here is certainly a woman who has taken her liberal arts education in a new direction she created for herself.

Let's close this discussion on the advantages your education has given you with some marvelous insights and advice from a highly respected professional educator and nonprofit corporate leader. David Clune demonstrates in his career the agility to move in many directions within a chosen professional calling because of his knowledge of what mattered to him in terms of a lifestyle and his educational foundation. He has been a schoolteacher, a school administrator, and the superintendent of an outstanding public school system. Currently he serves as President of the Educational Records Bureau, which designs and administers academic achievement and ability tests at all levels of schooling. We doubt that any college graduate has not taken some level of ERB testing in their earlier school life. David has won many awards for his performance and service to the public through his leadership in education. Those who know him well understand that his success is in large measure the result of his passion for his work and his natural talents that led him to his calling. Here is David's advice.

* * *

We mere mortals of bygone years, boomers and members of the silent generation, had to weave our own tapestry one thread at a time, not knowing for sure where the individual threads would take us, yet we knew we had to make multiple informed choices, oftentimes in the crucible of competing and conflicting priorities. The key question, of course, was what would be the basis for making those choices. Then, as now, we were forever torn between the morning and night of our desires, between what we needed and what we wanted. As the first in our family to earn a college degree, let alone an advanced degree, there wasn't a path to follow—new trails needed to be cut. Our needs were many and our wants were few. Public college was the only option. That was the easy part.

While hindsight is always 20/20, it is clear now that solid middle-class values, instilled by hard-working and supportive parents, were the lights that illuminated my life choices. Sound values guided my most important choice, of a spouse. Even though some important career choices were serendipitous at best and accidental at worst, mentors appeared in my life at crucial times to assist in life choices and helped shape a decision to pursue a career in education. They listened and asked provocative questions. They took a personal interest. They provided feedback. They shared their critical career choices and their life circumstances at the time. They helped me realize that education was important to me and helped float my boat, and I wanted to do the same for others. I relished the opportunity to make things work better in education.

Advice I would offer to college students and young graduates as they seek their calling and build their careers is as follows:

- Choose a college wisely, but choose a wise spouse even more wisely.

- It is not so much the college you get into that's important; it's what you get out of the college experience that counts in the long run.

- The giving that is invested in others provides a much greater return than an exclusive investment in self.

- Cutting new trails is more rewarding than following paths.

- Love expressed in deeds means much more than altruistic and clearly articulated yet unfulfilled intentions.

- Embrace teaching as a learner, whatever your chosen career; lead as a follower and in so doing set the feet of many on the trails of life.

- Lead in a way that enriches both today and thousands of tomorrows.

- Embrace a calling rather than doing a job; a calling that nurtures others by making their care your concern.

- Nurture the minds of those entrusted to your care, but equally important, help them mind their hearts and souls.

- Do not let the possibility of failure spoil any opportunity for success.

- Things that matter the least must not stand in the way of what matters the most, and what matters the most is that the future is in the hands, hearts, and minds of those on whose behalf you work each day.

- Develop a sound moral compass so that when confronted with the worst the world has to offer you won't be overwhelmed and when presented with the best you won't be led astray.

- Remember to laugh often and often at yourself; share your thrills of victory and agonies of defeat, your defining moments and moments of truth, your war stories and stories of worry, and your milestones and your millstones!

COMBINING YOUR NATURAL ABILITIES AND YOUR LIBERAL ARTS

What lessons can be learned from the stories of this group of individuals who have found their calling in some of the most interesting and stimulating and ever-changing callings? Clearly they have used their natural abilities together with their tool kit of skills, the Key Habits of Mind, and their passion for a particular cause or career. Fear of failure would not have gotten them to their present situations, nor would the lack of self-examination and determination.

Now it's on to that most dreaded subject of all: the Real World. Frankly, we think the distinction between a real world and some idyllic version of the "ivory tower" is overdrawn. Most of you probably had a number of real world experiences before and during college, and we suspect that many of you graduates reading this book have already hit the bright light of day and the challenges of the working world illuminated by it. Nevertheless, there are some genuine differences between college life and the demands of the working world, and we'd like to identify some of them here.

3

THE (NEXT) REAL WORLD

WE WANT TO TAKE ISSUE with the phrase that is so frequently referenced when addressing students, namely, that you need to prepare for the Real World that awaits you after completing your formal education. You and we know that the Real World is now, this moment and every day that you are on this earth doing what you can to learn about yourself and the immediate and larger world around you. You could not have completed your college education or (be about to do so) without treating each day as serious business socially as well as academically. You have lived in a world of reality from the moment you arrived on your college campus.

THE REAL COLLEGE WORLD

We commend you for carrying out successfully your time in school, where your real world has centered around the demands of your academic responsibilities, your engagement in clubs, sports, leadership training; where you have learned to coexist in an intense community of peers of many different personalities, viewpoints, and levels of approachability. You earned your diploma by figuring out over time how to cope with the demands of so many tests to prepare for, papers to be researched and written, books to be read and comprehended, while at the same time giving your best efforts on the athletic field, on the stage and studio, and in your various leadership roles. Time management became a survival skill, and if you were concerned enough you figured this out before you landed in serious academic trouble like so many of your classmates.

Oh, yes, and there was the matter of coping with the shock of collegiate freedom, adjusting to strange and sometimes questionable dietary offerings, adapting to roommates with entirely different habits within the walls of a room the size of your closet at home. You had to overcome bouts of loneliness, of sadness that could descend suddenly when you were least prepared for them. You have had to decide whether to tell your parents that all was not going well or that you needed them at a particular moment. We will not even broach the emotional highs and lows of that first romantic relationship with a schoolmate and how you coped. Most challenging of all, perhaps, you discovered that you were not necessarily the brightest student in your classes.

Your time in college very likely was spent surviving all-nighters in order to meet academic demands; making hundreds of seemingly small decisions that had major results, such as: Am I going to get out of bed and get to that early morning class? Am I going to get to the library and put quality time into that paper that needs to be completed? Am I going to study for a major exam and leave time to study again before the test? Am I going to turn on my computer and play video games or instant-message my friends instead of starting that paper or research project that is due soon? Am I going to block out time to get to the gym to work out or practice my lines for the play? Am I going to blow off my papers and exams and get wasted? Or am I going to take a bunch of gut courses that will enable me to pass with little effort?

And then there is the overarching, ever-present concern for what are you going to do when you graduate and, if you are in the same situation as over one half of your fellow students, how you will ever pay back the student loans and other debts you have incurred in order to get this education and diploma?

If this is not a Real World challenge, then what is? And where is it? If we as parents and future employers could muster the courage to relive similar experiences from our own youth, we would surprise you by our stories of similar emotional pendulum swings and confusion as to where our futures lay. By now in your young adult life you have figured out that the adults who have nourished and supported you are not perfect, that they, too, had to master the art of living in an intense school world and beyond. Few, if any of us, knew from day one exactly who we were, how we were to manage our lives with some small measure of dignity and grace, and what we were going to do with our adult lives!

LIFE AFTER COLLEGE IS DIFFERENT

But it is time for a serious reality check. For all of these challenges inherent in completing college, going out into the world of work is radically different in a critical aspect that defines success or possible failure for the college graduate. Your college experience was fundamentally based on a philosophy and an attitude of "We are here to serve you and to do all that we, the administration and faculty, can do to make your learning environment as positive as possible. You are here to learn much about yourself and the ideas and ideals that have shaped our civilization. We will do all that we can to support you in your journey of exploration and learning. We want you to take your time to experiment with new ideas, new interests, and new ways of thinking and learning.

We want you to be happy and comfortable while on this journey. Let us know what we can do for you to make this happen. We have advisers, counselors, coaches, deans, and learning experts to make your time with us happy and productive."

Can you imagine a corporation expected by its shareholders to think this way? Or a startup trying to survive its rocky road from idea to actual company and to repay its investors? Or a legal firm expected to produce positive results for its clients? Or a medical practice that calls for constant training in the latest findings in its field and service on demand from its patients? Or a nonprofit entity that is struggling financially to meet its budget while serving all kinds of people in need of some sort of assistance? Or a technical firm that has to produce major projects on a tight time line in a severely competitive market? None of these would have the same attitude as your college. And yet, for so many graduates starting out in the world of work, this is a transition not easily carried out. We are all creatures of habit, especially when the habits we have grown accustomed to are enjoyable and rewarding ones. All too often this dramatic difference is lost in the initial stages of joining a particular workplace.

Now the business and professional and service people in charge are saying, "What can you contribute to our enterprise and how will you adapt yourself to our needs and our goals? We expect you to join the present team and learn as much as you can as quickly as you can in order to make a tangible benefit to our company. The burden is on you to demonstrate what your potential is for learning and contributing to a cause larger than yourself. We are not here to satisfy your curiosity or your basic needs or build your self-esteem. Now is the time to demonstrate to us that you have the personal qualities and the ability to learn through your performance." Remember those key personal qualities employers in all the various kinds of enterprises have identified as marking the successful employee. These are not the same as specialized skills or aptitudes. They include:

INTERPERSONAL SKILLS: The ability to interact in a positive and understanding way with fellow workers and managers. No longer is life about you and what you want, or what you will choose to take advantage of on your own terms, as you were able to from your college's people and resources.

A TEAMWORK ATTITUDE: If you played a sport or sang in a choral group, performed in the theater, served as a class officer, or ran a community service program on campus, you understand why teamwork is critical to success. This holds as true or truer in any of the business, technical, or professional fields you enter.

A STRONG WORK ETHIC: While this may seem like an obvious requirement for success, the definition of what constitutes a serious attitude toward work may vary greatly from the college to the workplace. Supervisors may expect or demand that you spend unlimited hours to complete an assignment or oversee a project. This includes working evenings or weekends when necessary to get the job done.

INHERENT MOTIVATION AND INITIATIVE: No longer are you doing just enough to pass a course or finish a paper. Now you are expected to take initiative and find every opportunity to help see a project through to completion, or to service a client, or find a solution to a problem. Motivation to get the job done in a timely and productive manner is the engine that drives the enterprise. Friends, dorm advisers, deans, and faculty are not there to remind you of what you have to get done or to excuse you for any reasons you might consider reasonable.

SOCIAL AND EMOTIONAL MATURITY: Who did not undergo a significant degree of maturing during our college years? That is, in large measure, what college is intended to do. The work world has a different attitude: It expects you to demonstrate your maturity on all fronts. What does this mean? Everything from committing wholeheartedly to a position you have assumed; taking full responsibility for what you do or fail to do in fulfilling your assignments; showing up every day and on time as required (no excuses, thank you very much); communicating orally and in writing in a mature language and tone rather than the casual, cool, clipped language of the college community or the Internet; putting your "attitudes" on the shelf and recognizing the mission and goals of the organization with which you have signed on; and separating personal issues from professional responsibilities while on the job. Many of the essential qualities mentioned here that will lead to success in whatever calling you will ultimately choose require a large measure of social and emotional maturation. We include in this category the ability to defer your gratification, to delay satisfying your personal needs until you have accomplished those tasks assigned to you by others. You would not have gotten yourself into college and out the other end if you had not developed this ability. However, you are more likely to find that you need to take this to another level in your work environment since more will be expected of you and the options to choose what you want to do at a particular moment are less elastic.

PERSEVERANCE: It is very likely that you developed this critical characteristic during your college days. This is the trait that got you through some tough courses, helped you win a spot on a team or an election for class officer as a few of hundreds of examples. Organizational leaders in all fields seem always to refer to the outstanding worker who had this quality of sticking with an assignment, no matter the obstacles or times of frustration, to finally meet the desired goal.

ADAPTABILITY AND RESILIENCY: An expression that was once popular was borrowed from the world of boxing, namely "rolling with the punches." Every day at work you can be confronted with frustration over the job that you cannot get done the way you want. Perhaps your employer tells you that a new plan has been put in place and you need to abort all the work you have done recently. Or you are assigned to a new project or position or the funding your group had counted on to meet the goals of the group has evaporated. Adapting to any and all of these changes is a requisite for keeping your sanity and success in finding other ways and means to accomplish your goals. Resiliency means rolling with the punches rather than taking a knockout blow directly on the chin.

Thomas Friedman, journalist and author of *The World Is Flat*, has written of a "quiet crisis" in America and American education. Part of the complex problem he identifies is a certain amount of complacency and personal protectionism. From an early age in school, children are protected from failing and are not held to the highest international standards. This holds true as our high school graduates enter college often unprepared for the work and competition present in any good collegiate environment. If you succeeded in graduating college, and perhaps you encountered some real academic and intellectual challenges for the first time. Once you enter the next real world, you should be prepared for even more exposure to the "flat world" where, increasingly, highly educated competitors in India, China, Japan, the former Soviet Block countries of Eastern Europe, and other nations are challenging American companies and American workers by being better educated, harder working, more committed, and hungrier to succeed. If you think you are insulated from these global challenges by dint of your college education, Friedman presents a strong argument as to why you need to watch out for your own career in the world marketplace.

Dede Bartlett, a liberal arts graduate of Vassar College, built a successful career in corporate America at a time when women were still kept far below the metaphorical glass ceiling of leadership positions. As a senior officer with two Fortune 25 companies, she acquired the skill sets necessary to attain her goals. Today she lectures to college-age students around the country on what she calls the ABCs of workplace behavior, or how to survive in your first job. We share with you here her advice that can help you in making the transition from the college environment to the work world. Much of her sound counsel appeared in a guest column for *University Business Magazine*'s August 2006 issue.

DEDE BARTLETT'S ABCs OF WORKPLACE BEHAVIOR

THE BASICS, OR UNLEARNING ACQUIRED HABITS

a. **Punctuality and face time.** Know when to arrive for work, when to leave, and how much time to spend with your colleagues and supervisor. Every organization has its own unwritten expectations of "face time" at the office.

b. **E-mail etiquette.** Employers complain regularly about the e-mail writing of many of their employees, as they often use poor speech and grammar and an overly informal writing style. E-mail messages should be written in a professional manner. All personal messaging should be done away from the office. These basic rules hold true for telephone and cell communications.

c. **Keep your personal and professional lives separate.** The workplace is not the same as the dorm or the social center on campus, where you could openly discuss your dating issues or any personal problems you might be having. If you are listed on Facebook or MySpace, be very careful about what information you post. It is now a common practice for prospective employers to check out a potential employee's site for more insight about the candidate.

d. **Dress.** Inappropriate clothing is another complaint of employers. Start out with a conservative wardrobe. You cannot embarrass yourself this way. Observe how your colleagues dress and even ask your boss what is the proper attire.

BEHAVIOR

a. **Be a team player.** Organizations put a high premium on teamwork and team players.

b. **Be enthusiastic and congenial.** Present a can-do attitude and leave your temper or negative feelings at home.

c. **Accept responsibility for your work.** If you make a mistake, admit it and learn from the experience.

d. **Volunteer.** You will learn and be recognized by volunteering for specific assignments and special projects.

e. **Ask questions.** Tell your supervisor you do not understand something you have been asked to do. You are not expected to know very much as a new worker and asking is the only way to learn. You will be respected for this attitude and you will likely be given more responsibilities accordingly.

STRATEGY

a. **Listen and observe.** Analyze the culture in which you are working. You need to understand the way people behave and how the organization functions and then adapt yourself accordingly. Failure to do this will make the job difficult and likely that it will not last very long.

b. **Work closely with your employer and help him to do his job well.** This is a key function in your position. Do not undercut or circumvent him. You will learn from both a good and a bad boss and this will influence how you will manage others in the future.

c. **Find a personal mentor within the organization.** Identify a person who is well respected and with whom you feel a natural relationship can be formed. The right mentor can teach a good deal about the culture of the organization and how to build your career.

Dede speaks to the facts of life in the work world today. The odds are higher than ever that you could be fired from your first or second job. The competition on a global scale has made job security tenuous as more work is outsourced to other countries, and company downsizing and mergers have become a necessity for survival. Many of the most successful people in all fields note that their ultimate path to finding their calling came as the result of losing their job early in their career. Steve Jobs, who founded Apple Computer, once told the graduating seniors at Stanford that "getting fired from Apple was the best thing that could have ever happened to me. The heaviness of being successful was replaced by the lightness of being a beginner again, less sure about everything. It freed me to enter one of the most creative periods of my life." Eventually, Jobs returned as CEO of Apple and took the company to new heights of success based on new products that he helped create.

Scott Meadow holds the dual titles of Director of Global Academic Initiatives and Professor of Entrepreneurship at the University of Chicago Graduate School of Business. He has been recognized officially many times for his excellence in teaching by his students and university. Scott brings over 25 years of experience in venture capital and private equity firms to his teaching and advising. He is a liberal arts graduate of Harvard, where he also received his MBA. He is a thoughtful, talented individual who has much of note to share with young adults starting out in their work.

MY CALLING TO TEACH. As a scholarship student during secondary school and college, I was called on to do odd jobs and wait on my fellow students. Therefore, in the early days of my career, I was highly motivated by the prestige factor. A huge mistake. I enjoyed the creativity of my business career, the notion that I was enhancing the lives of thousands of employees, and the financial rewards, but out of some fifty partners that I have had in my various ventures, there are only five with whom I would want to have dinner on Saturday night. Teaching has been a wonderful addition to my life. Some people build a legacy by erecting a building in their honor. I am building my legacy brick by brick, with each brick being a student who has sat in my classroom or has come by my office for counsel. So far I have made over 4,000 bricks.

MY CAREER PLANNING IN THE EARLY STAGES. Planning is better cast as "disciplined, systematized experimentation." This view of planning a calling or a life's work begins with dipping into courses and jobs that provide insight and preparation for a potential career. If you are still in college, the course selection will be more focused as summer jobs help to sharpen your interest level to follow a particular path. The considered life generally leads to a state, to paraphrase the ancient sages, where "one is wealthy who is satisfied with one's portion." For every individual, that path to a considered life will be a different path and it is likely to evolve over time as one settles into that state of satisfaction.

THE PRESENT REALITY IN THE WORK WORLD. The old rules do not apply anymore in the business world. It used to be if you changed jobs after two years you were stigmatized as a "job hopper." In the first half of 2008, Wall Street firms "downsized" by 35,000 jobs. Clearly, most business entities have no qualms today about "hopping" from employee to employee as financial circumstances change. Therefore, why should the graduate be concerned about treating every job as a residency that allows them to advance their own level of confidence, depth, and breadth of knowledge about a field, while enhancing his professionalism and self-confidence? In the end, one must be loyal first to one's own development, because it is that depth of knowledge and the resulting self-confidence that will provide security. Paternalism and job security from one's employer are things of the past.

Scott presents a pretty strong case for making the most you can out of your early positions as a learning and developmental growth experience, while recognizing that the majority of for-profit enterprises are not bound to a culture of loyalty and long-term support of their employees. This is played out against a background of the "flat world" economy, where competition in the for-profit sectors has become a global affair. Every business has to find continually more efficient and thus less costly methods of doing business. The individual worker is most often the piece of the business plan that is sacrificed as fewer employees are asked to do the work that many carried out previously. This is a harsh reality, but you need to be fully aware of this as you venture into your first jobs. The skill sets and attributes we have described above are your best tools for succeeding in your first experiences out of college. In time, you will move on through the labyrinth to find that right fit for yourself.

FACING PERSONAL CHALLENGES IN THE NEXT REAL WORLD

Many college graduates will experience significant personal and financial challenges as they leave the college nest. You might be handling a real budget for the first time; or managing significant increases in expenses as you move from college housing or low-rent off-campus accommodations, or from your parents' house to a rental apartment in a major metropolitan area. If you have college loans, the repayment period has begun or will soon do so. This can take up a substantial amount of the discretionary income from an entry-level job's salary. What if you have health issues, personal counseling concerns, worries over safety and security in your living or work environment, or substance abuse challenges?

For these and many other reasons, an increasing number of

college grads seem to be returning to their parents' houses for a few months or even a few years. Sometimes this can work to your advantage as you search for a job, apply to graduate schools, or save a few bucks. In other cases, such renewed dependency can stifle your learning curve and personal growth. While we are not arguing against moving in with your folks in every case (personal experience would make us unwise to do so!), we caution you not to use the availability of this option as a crutch. Seek to move forward in your career planning and personal independence as soon as you can, using your home base, if you are fortunate enough to have a good one, as a refuge, refueling station, and source of comfort, rather than a semi-permanent solution to a lack of direction or progress.

In addition to your parents or extended family, there are many resources available to you to help you handle bumps in the road. You will just need to be more assertive, proactive, and creative in seeking them out. For student loans, there are loan consolidation programs as well as loan forgiveness options associated with certain career choices.

You can also talk to an accountant or financial adviser about how to plan your finances and what will work best for you in terms of tax, savings, and retirement planning options. In a later chapter we will talk about nonprofit and governmental work opportunities that might also impact your student loan situation.

From professional counseling options to lower-cost human service agencies, community mediation and counseling programs, and substance-abuse treatment groups like Alcoholics

LOAN FORGIVENESS

See these links for more information on public service and teacher loan forgiveness, for example:

- www.nasfaa.org/publications/2007/lnpublic101507.html
- studentaid.ed.gov/PORTALSWebApp/students/english/cancelstaff.jsp

Anonymous, there are many resources available to you, and we encourage you to take advantage of them if you feel yourself getting overwhelmed by personal or other challenges you will face after leaving college. There can be many: problems with roommates or romantic partners; eating disorders; serious illness; mental health disorders; learning disabilities; financial crises; crime victimization; the loss of a parent or sibling; difficulties adapting to a new living environment. You are not immune to any of these concerns just because you are smart and graduated with a college degree. And, you are not alone. It is likely that you have classmates and friends who are confronting some of the same difficulties. Access your resources and use your friends and family to help you through these difficulties earlier rather than later so you can move forward with your life.

4

NETWORKING TO FIND YOUR PATH

NETWORKING. EVERYONE HAS HEARD THE term. What does it mean? How does a well-educated student or graduate identify and create a network? How do you use a network? What is social capital? Networking is an essential skill and habit that does not come naturally to everyone, and we can all become better networkers over the years. Networking is something you must work at. If done well, it can help you develop internship and job opportunities, as well as friendships and community bonds that will last a lifetime.

Today networking takes place on a constant basis among

your generation of computer natives—Facebookers who spend so much time communicating with friends near and far from various stages of your lives. Colleges and companies are seeking to tap into these networks to find well-educated and well-qualified recruits. You can use your online networks and your networks through your college, current workplace, or friends and family to open up possible internships or job choices.

BASIC NETWORKING SKILL REQUIREMENTS

Let's not assume anything, though. If you are not skilled with a computer and the use of the Internet, or if you are unfamiliar with e-mailing, instant messaging, Googling, and accessing social networking sites, then you need to concentrate on building this set of skills immediately. Do you need to know HTML and Java programming languages? No. But you do need to know how to navigate the Internet, use a variety of search tools, establish Web pages and create a page on MySpace, Facebook, LinkedIn, or other social and business networking sites. And, as Dede Bartlett suggested earlier, know when and how to separate your personal and professional lives in cyberspace networks, where your information is widely accessible.

The other element to reiterate is that you should e-mail in a professional manner. That's right. We said "professional manner." You might be the best two-thumbed texter spelling out the latest jargon, but if you send a résumé and cover letter to a prospective employer, to a faculty member requesting a reference letter, or to a fellow alum from your college asking for an informational interview, and use that casual texting style—CULA! (That's "see you later, alligator," for the uninitiated.) Computers, e-mail, and the Internet have helped us all write more and more frequently, but not always with the best spelling and grammar. Most professionals and those over 30 are likely using e-mail today, but not instant messaging or text messages as much, especially when communicating on work-related matters. You won't necessarily need to send hard copies by snail mail when networking, but you will need to compose well-written, mature e-mails if you want to be taken seriously.

If you need help learning the cyberspace ropes, there are abundant courses and workshops available on college campuses, at local community colleges, and at local computer stores. Many are also accessible online. Take advantage of these classes, which are often free or very low in cost, to build your tech skills and you won't be left behind to miss out on valuable networking opportunities.

Communication skills should be attributes you developed in your education, and now is the time you will need to utilize them to your best ability. This includes the technical skills essential to operating in today's Internet world, as well as the reading, writing, and speaking skills we discussed in chapter 2. A major form of networking will be communicating through phone calls, e-mails, over lunches, at coffees, and social or community organizations. Research and information gathering will help you discover and develop your networks. If you need work on how you present yourself, your college career services office might offer workshops that can assist you in making public presentations, writing key letters, and, yes, having a business lunch.

For additional work on some of these networking skills, such organizations as Toastmasters International (www.toastmasters.org) and Dale Carnegie Training (www.dalecarnegie.com) offer resource materials and courses to help you improve your performance.

KENNETH WACHTEL ON THE IMPORTANCE OF NETWORKING

A former senior executive at Excite@Home and CBS Television Network, Kenneth Wachtel was a Government and Economics major at Dartmouth who earned an MBA at the University of Chicago. Today he runs his own executive recruiting consultancy and works with individuals on career planning. His comments on networking and finding your calling are well worth remembering.

MY GRANDFATHER AND FATHER WERE both involved in marketing and sales, so it is in my blood. Other than sports, as a young boy in the 1950s and '60s, television was the major medium, so my interest in communications, coupled with my marketing knowledge and sales ability, helped lead me to my career. In business, I always developed a strong personal network, and dealt fairly, honestly, and respectably with every business associate, both internal and external. I kept in touch with everyone on a regular basis, particularly my most important contacts. I also was tremendously involved with each person who worked for me—training, nurturing, and mentoring a ton of younger talent throughout their jobs and careers. I always felt that raising the people beneath me, indirectly raised me as well—that my own success was built on the successes of others.

Very few people I worked for in my career operated the same way; they were almost all out for themselves. I was told early on in my career that the same people that you meet on the way up, you will see again on the way down, so treat everyone equally well. It is no accident that I ended up in my own business, with an informal network of acquaintances that have made my personal executive recruiting business interesting and successful. I never worried about title and money; I figured that if I did well, and the company recognized my achievement, that the titles and money would follow, which they did. What matters most to me is that I am excited to wake up every day and go to work. If I do not have that, I have nothing.

I would advise students and graduates to find the area where both your abilities and interests coincide. If you are good at something but have no interest, or if you are interested in something but have no ability, neither of these situations will yield an optimal choice. The combination of heightened interest and significant ability would yield a more desirable result. Also, you need to figure out how important money and the pursuit of it is in your life, so you can maintain your desired standard of living. Working as a teacher and owning five homes might not be possible.

Expand your personal network of people: Visit them at work, and discuss their careers and what they have learned, their likes and dislikes. Don't be afraid to include your parents, your parents' friends, and the parents of your friends in order to get the best set of contacts and entrees into your chosen line of work. No one remembers after six months in the job how you landed the job, or through what set of contacts. Speak to college alums who are already in your line of work, both for informational interviews as well as more serious discussions.

UTILIZING ALUMNI NETWORKS

Remember that career services office? There and in your college's alumni relations office you will find a major source of networking information. Additional college-based networks include fraternity or sorority organizations, sports teams, clubs, secret or honor societies, and even academic departments that are maintaining their own newsletters and lists of graduates. A cold call or e-mail to a new contact is a lot warmer when you can identify a common reference point like sharing the same alma mater.

Much of the informal college-based networking has been moving online in recent years, with Facebook and other sites allowing you to join networks based on college, high school, graduate school, Greek organization, sports, or other affiliations. Nevertheless, connecting with your college's core network is an important foundation for your future contacts. In many instances, you can list your own affiliations and interests and offer to serve as a mentor or information source for current and future graduates, thus continuing the cycle. What we have found over the years is that the longer you are out of college, the less the year in which you graduated matters. Whether you went to an elite liberal arts college, a giant flagship public university, or a small regional institution, what will be important over time is the connection to the same institution, not who you were when you attended or when you got your first job.

In your community or region, another stop you should consider is joining your college's alumni club. Such organizations host meetings, promote social and volunteer service activities, and facilitate admissions recruiting efforts. Alumni clubs are a great way to meet graduates of your college of many ages and at many stages.

DEVELOPING COMMUNITY NETWORKS

This is a broad category, but often overlooked by young college graduates. There is a reason that organizations like Rotary International, Kiwanis, Lions, Elks, Masons, and other clubs and fraternal societies have been around so long on Main Street. Combining volunteer service and social activities, they connect members with one another and with local, national, and international colleagues. Many young residents of small towns and large cities are returning to these organizations to set down roots in their communities and establish important contacts.

Similar networks can be established through local Chambers of Commerce, the Better Business Bureau, and various professional organizations and unions. For those interested in community service, getting involved with nonprofit organizations and volunteer service activities will help you to make a difference locally and beyond. From local human service agencies to advocacy organizations like the American Civil Liberties Union, the national and state Public Interest Research Groups, the National Association for the Advancement of Colored People, the Audubon Society, or the Sierra Club, you should be able to find a cause and an organization (or several) that fit you. You'll also meet like-minded individuals with diverse backgrounds and build on interests you may have established in high school and college. As we'll discuss later, you might even find a way to do well by doing good and discover that your future lies within the not-for-profit sphere.

If you have children, schools—whether public or private—are another venue for connecting with your community. We're not suggesting using schools for your own benefit in a crass manner. Rather, we are encouraging you to get involved. Schools provide a major source of networking for many young families, and you never know whom you'll meet. If you are new to a community, school involvement can be one of the easiest and best ways to make connections and feel at home. The same holds true for religious organizations. If religion is important to you, or is becoming more so especially as you start a family, sampling some of the religious groups in your area is a good way to find a community that fits your faith and personal and family values.

Country clubs, athletic clubs, and sports leagues are another source of connections. In some cases, you might need to be a resident of a town or city for some period of time to build up the relationships that will help you join an exclusive club. In most instances, you will be able to join a low-key club; participate on a softball, basketball, or soccer league; or go to the local YMCA. These are all things you probably took for granted in college, but in that "real world" we have been discussing, you'll need to be more proactive about establishing these communities for yourself. They will be important to your own well-being and enjoyment, and a natural by-product over time, classic networking opportunities.

Finally, political involvement is another way to network

locally as well as at the state and national level. You might be part of a national party or movement with a local branch just begging for leadership and energy. You could consider using your talents by running for a local selectman or city council seat, or serving on a board of finance, education, or planning. Again, you'll make a difference in something you care about while simultaneously forming networks across a variety of areas.

USING INTERNSHIPS TO YOUR ADVANTAGE

How do internships help talented graduates realize their interests and position themselves for their ideal career? Whether during college, just after graduation, or at some point during a career shift, part- or full-time (low) paid or volunteer internships have become a crucial stepping stone on the path to exploring and perhaps entering a career field or a particular organization. It is likely that you have had some sort of internship during high school, college, or thereafter. Internships are as important as ever, and we encourage you to keep them in mind as possibilities as you consider your career planning.

High school internships can help you explore some career interests or aptitudes, gain some experience, mature developmentally, and put together a nice résumé for college admissions. Yet they are unlikely to seem particularly relevant to you later in your college years or thereafter. In college, internships can be key elements in exploring career fields and making contacts in industries of interest to you. As the banking contraction of 2008 has shown, those who had a strong internship experience in an investment banking position, for example, were more likely to get a post-graduation job from that bank. Legal internships can help with law school applications, just as medically oriented internships and volunteer activities can assist with medical college admissions.

Internships help you build your résumé. Just as important, they help you discover which career fields are more or less of interest to you, and which areas within those industries or careers are most appropriate for your skills and interests. You might get an internship as a result of your networking activities, and then build your network through your internship experience. Internships are generally low-risk ways to explore job possibilities, and proving yourself during the internship is a tried-and-true way to land yourself a full-time position.

It is easier to take advantage of internship opportunities when you are younger. You likely have less to lose by taking on a three-month to one-year position; moving to a new city; working for very low pay or for free; or trying out a new career path. Later on, you might have a family to worry about or a significant investment in a local community. If you're a college student looking to direct an off-campus experience or fill up your summer productively, an internship is a natural choice. If you're exploring law, teaching, or architecture, a short-term internship could be just the path to help you reach a decision on applying for full-time work or to a graduate degree program in this field.

How do you get an internship? Aren't they as competitive as getting a job? Yes and no. Some are designed specifically for young college graduates without a lot of experience, and are offered by employers as low-risk and low-cost ways for them to discover and develop new talent. Teaching internships at boarding schools are examples of this. Others, such as those at high-profile banks, law firms, or consultancies, are selective, so you will want to apply to those organizations that seem to be looking for individuals with your set of skills and talents. Your career services office, as well as online resources like Monster.com, can help link you to internships that fit.

Finally, you could seek to create an internship where one doesn't already exist. We recently employed an intern in our small office who contacted us of her own accord, seeking to gain experience in the field of educational consulting. We had not advertised a position nor had we defined such a job, but in writing and talking with this college student we discovered that she was looking at us for the right reasons, that we could help her discover whether this field was appropriate for her future, and that she could help us with some specific projects in which we were engaged. Similar stories abound of students connecting with architectural firms, fashion designers, photographers, veterinarians, auctioneers, museums, web designers, magazine and book publishers, politicians, and others. Use your network to contact someone working in a field of interest to you, and ask if they have positions available. If they don't, propose creating one, and ask for an informational interview to get your foot in the door.

INTERVIEWING FOR INFORMATION

Perhaps a company you are interested in does not have a job opening. Perhaps a contact you have made works in a field that sounds intriguing. Informational interviewing plays a vital role in researching a career path and following your Thread. Most people are flattered when contacted by an earnest college student or graduate asking for some time to talk about what they do for a living. If you have a specific network connection—an alumni relationship, a reference from a friend or family member, or a relationship based on a community organization—then you will have an easier time gaining some interview time. Cold calls (or e-mails) still do work effectively, however.

When asking for an informational interview, you are not pushing for a job. You will want to use this time effectively to learn about what the person does, how he got to where he is, and what Threads he followed to reach his current position. As your learning curve expands, you will begin to see whether this career seems to fit your interests and strengths. If it is apparent that a potential match exists, you might take the opportunity to follow up with your contact to propose an internship experience. That is, if she has not already connected you with a job or several other people you can talk with, which is often the case.

With informational interviewing, it is important to use your best communications etiquette. Your résumé and cover letter should be carefully written and proofread, your language fairly formal, and your reasons for wanting to talk clear. You should thank your contact after the interview with a more relaxed but still professional e-mail. This discussion may not have borne fruit, but these contacts have a way of multiplying over time to lead to opportunities further down the line.

CREATING THE JOB YOU WANT

Creativity in following your Thread is an essential aspect of finding your calling. If your ideal job or career doesn't exist, maybe you can create it. Inventiveness can inspire. We can see this at work quite readily if we consider Bill Gates recognizing the importance of software for the future of computing; or Steve Jobs and Steve Wozniak tinkering in a garage to found Apple Computer; Larry Page and Sergey Brin creating Google; David Filo and Jerry Yang founding Yahoo!; or the many other examples from the Internet age.

Yet we can also see inventiveness and creativity exemplified in the stories of Oprah Winfrey, Wendy Kopp (founder of Teach for America), Ted Halstead (founder of the New America Foundation), or Rick Rubin and Russell Simmons (founders of Def Jam Recordings). Many thousands of other examples can be found across America and around the world, and it is what keeps our economy vibrant and renewed. If you see a niche for yourself, a passion that doesn't seem to have an outlet, one of the clear lessons from all of our contributors to the book is *Go for it!*

5

BALANCING RISK AND REWARD

A .300 hitter would hit his pitch every time, but as often as not when the .280 hitter would get his pitch, he'd foul it off. The same difference seems to be true of most of what we attempt in life. . . . When the time comes just two things matter: How well prepared we are to seize the moment and having the courage to take our best swing.

—HANK AARON, THE GREAT BASEBALL HOME RUN KING,
SPEAKING AT EMORY UNIVERSITY

ARE YOU A RISK TAKER by nature? Do you tend to look for that right pitch and not hesitate to swing when you get it? How important to you is security? What is your personal definition of security: Being good enough to do an assigned task or job satisfactorily or working in an environment where there is little chance of being let go or there is the prospect of earning a steady income and benefits? What is your threshold for taking chances that could result in either disappointment or failure? To be sure, one of the telltale signs of the "new economy" is a lack of predictability due to constant change and thus a sense of risk inherent in almost every occupation. Every study of the state of our economy, which includes a breakdown job loss by education, shows that college graduates have the least exposure to loss of jobs and unemployment, thanks to their skills and ability to learn and adapt. Nevertheless, you are reading this guide because you are not interested in landing just any job at any cost to your psyche; rather you want to find your way to work, to find work that will become your calling. This will involve risk taking as you weave your way through the labyrinth.

TAKING A RISK

What do we mean by risk taking, and why will you have to become a risk taker at various moments in your life to arrive at your goal? Simply put, you are going to make choices that could potentially have unexpected consequences. If you were to interview leaders in any of your potential fields of interest and ask them how they reached their present position, you are very likely to hear stories about risks: the chances they took along the way by choosing one internship or job opportunity over another: opting to go to graduate school or choosing not to continue their formal education; leaving a secure situation in order to move to another position that appeared to provide a better opportunity to learn and take on more responsibility. Every person we interviewed for this book commented on those points at which—as they worked their way through their personal labyrinth—they had to take a risk. As the oft-quoted phrase has it, "It goes with the territory."

Thomas Friedman's book *The World Is Flat* presents a coherent picture of the way things are getting done at an ever-increasing pace in an expanding global economy. Both the private for-profit and not-for-profit sectors that sustain our society need to adapt continually and take more risks as there are fewer guaranteed outcomes and less stability in a complex, interconnected society. While your personal decisions on what you want to do with your life at any given time center on your interests, abilities, and needs, you must understand the larger playing field in which you will be a participant.

In chapter 2, "The Liberal Artist Goes to Work," we reviewed the key ingredients are for realizing successful outcomes in the workplace. Add to this list "developing the emotional capability and willingness to take chances at key points of opportunity in your young life." Of course, you will bring to these decision points much internal reflection on your longer-term goals and a realistic evaluation of your skill sets and interest level based on your more recent experiences. Friedman identifies, among the other traits we have discussed, the need to be an adapter in a volatile society. He likens this ability to training for the Olympics without knowing what sport you will eventually compete in.

The epic tale of Odysseus in Homer's *Odyssey* offers, in its own fashion, a theme as appropriate today as it was in ancient times. Odysseus represents personal courage, ingenuity, adaptability, and risk taking as he returns to his home in Ithaca after fighting for Greece against the city of Troy. His ten-year sojourn is a story of one challenge after another, requiring him to use all of his skills and wits to survive. Today we think of an *odyssey* as a journey of discovery and exposure to new challenges and risks (though generally much less life-threatening than those Odysseus had to contend with!). It's not as if Cyclops and Sirens and Lotus Eaters want to lure you to a cataclysmic ending.

Nevertheless, you are embarking on a journey that does not have a certain time line or even a guaranteed final destination. You should relish this opportunity to take chances by trying out different internships, paying positions, or community service, or by immersing yourself in the interest you have held dear for some time but have not had the window of time to commit to. What has been a passionate interest may well turn out to become your life's work, or it may prove to be more of a lifetime hobby. How do you know the rightness of your true commitments unless you set off on an odyssey of your own devising? You will do so while understanding and accepting that you may land in many unfamiliar settings that could prove incredibly exciting and long-lasting, or which will persuade you to set sail in another direction. Keeping with the navigational metaphor, your initial ports of call are not going to be your final destinations. Every experience should be perceived as a learning opportunity that clarifies still further your preferred direction in the long lifetime that lies ahead.

ELEMENTS OF BUILDING SUCCESS

We believe strongly in a handful of simple concepts that have helped direct our own lives and those of the many accomplished college graduates we know. See if these are ones that you can identify with and thus refer to as you reach key decision points that represent risk taking in the early stages of your odyssey to find your future calling:

- Belief in yourself and trust in your own instincts are essential elements to making choices, taking risks, and learning from each wrong path.

- Personal courage and persistence are essential to creating a future of your own choosing.

- Honesty with yourself as to what you genuinely care about, what your core values are, and what matters to you—and not the other people in your life—will lead you in the right direction.

- Competency leads to confidence, which leads to exploring different opportunities.

- Talent leads to passionate interests, which lead to boundless energy and a focus on eventual goals.

- Leading from your strengths and away from your weaknesses brings you personal satisfaction and thus success at your work. Focus on what you are good at, not the things you cannot do.

- Hard work in the early stages of exploring and experimenting will result in far greater satisfaction and success in finding your calling in time.

DEALING WITH RISK AVOIDANCE

By our very nature most of us are risk averse. Who wants to be out on that proverbial limb having been found wanting in ability or competency? How many times have you said, "I really want to try out for the baseball or soccer team or the chorus or the school play or a new job or a position of leadership"—and then persuaded yourself you are not up to it. The thought of looking foolish is too strong to allow you to take the risk. Conversely, how good does it feel to overcome your anxiety and push yourself to take that chance at succeeding and then actually do it? As you move through the labyrinth of building your future calling, consciously remind yourself of the times you succeeded when you put yourself out there. No event is too small to ignore. Each rewarding experience builds on the next and the next, to give you that foundation of confidence to take larger and larger chances that seem right for you. Make a list of every decision you have made up to now that had an element of risk or unknown consequences attached to it. In deciding what risks to take consider the guidelines we have listed here. And this way over time you will recognize the right pitch when it comes over the plate.

Feeling uncomfortable at times with the path you are on presently can be a good thing. It can force you to consider alternatives and start in a new direction. If you believe you have no other options you can become frozen and too fearful to make a move that will have consequences for you. We often suggest to the young adults we counsel to imagine the worst scenario that can happen when making a choice and taking a risk. Most of the time the worst scenario turns out to look fairly benign.

We think of a talented musician who graduated recently from Yale University with a concentration in English. She had her sights set on writing and performing folk and contemporary music that had personal and social statements attached to it. By spending several years trying to break into the professional music scene in New York, she realized that while she was an accomplished musician and writer, she wanted this part of her to remain more of a personal expressive outlet rather than her professional one. What she learned through living in a very low-rent district in lower Manhattan was that she was passionate about the plight of the many highly talented artists who were naive about financial and legal matters, and thus were at the mercy of the business people who controlled the commercial arts outlets.

She recognized then that what she really wanted to commit herself to was legal representation of young artists to help them deal on an equal playing field with the business interests in the music and other arts industries. Her goal also was to set up a foundation that would provide legal services to this particular group at little or no cost. She therefore decided to apply to law schools in order to carry out her newfound mission. Having majored in English at Yale, she was well prepared to cope with the heavy demands of a legal education. Her ability to read critically, to analyze complicated legal cases from several perspectives, and to write and speak coherently in her classes has made her a successful student. While the future will tell if her mission, which she refers to as her calling, will be completed, she definitely knows the direction in which she is headed. There are risks involved, but the rewards for her more than justify the effort.

Our society has a need to assign labels to individuals and what they think and how they act at particular historical periods of time. Certainly, the media use these catchall labels as they attempt to characterize, interpret, and predict the habits of these generalized groups. As a result, we are led to believe that all individuals in these groups have similar values, goals, and behavior patterns. In the last half century, we have had the baby boomers, generation X and Y, and the graying society, depending on someone's year of birth. More recently, a new term is being used to identify the population of young adults experiencing life in their twenties.

You may not have already heard this, if you are a twenty-something, you are considered to be traveling through your *odyssey* years. This is a life stage somewhere between adolescence and adulthood. What does this mean? Well, you are remaining for shorter periods in any one experience and taking longer than your parents to settle into a permanent career, to become totally financially independent, to get married and start a family, or to starting and complete graduate school or other professional training programs. As David Brooks wrote recently in the *New York Times*: "Yet with a little imagination it's possible even for baby boomers to understand what it's like to be in the middle of the odyssey years. It's possible to see that this period of improvisation is a sensible response to modern conditions. . . . And as the new generational structure solidifies, social and economic entrepreneurs will create new rites and institutions."

To many adults, most often parents, this odyssey phase is viewed with some concern. They worry if you will ever settle down in a "real job" that represents a steady course of future security, whether you will be fully independent (including not living at home or changing your address every several months), and when you will find that right other person. We, by contrast, consider this time of voyaging a wonderful opportunity to explore any and all interests that appeal to you and might lead you to your final destination. Truth be told, many of the generations that preceded you would like to have had more flexibility and time to explore a larger universe and to experiment in different roles before committing to their eventual lifestyle and work. We encounter many college students these days who have taken time out from their studies or have left their work to travel to different ports of the world or to volunteer in disadvantaged urban and rural communities or to attempt to make a successful career in the field of their passion.

JOHN McHALE'S STORY

John McHale has led a professional life that many people dream about. He is the Vice President of Major League Baseball. His demanding but exciting career did not start with this objective in mind, however. How he got to this role, which he enjoys immensely, illustrates much of what we suggest you consider as you head out on your journey. John shared with us the following personal story.

> I HAVE HAD 33 YEARS of phenomenally interesting professional life that has taken me from Washington, D.C., to Denver, then Detroit, and now to New York City. The first half of my working life was spent as a lawyer. The second half, from 1991 to today, has been spent as a part of Major League Baseball, a privilege unimaginable for all but a sliver of my sixteen years as a lawyer. The transition was the cul-

mination of a series of fortunate coincidences, many brought about by forces completely out of my control. Even my transitions within the halves do not seem particularly organic. The good ones, like the major transition of my professional life, seem now to be the result of being in the right place at the right time.

What I can see from here as I look backward across these three decades are three powerful forces that have accompanied me to my fortunate and happy present. They have to do with priorities, the incidental value of public service, and the importance of colleagues.

I have always been willing, and what's more important, able to take chances in my professional life. Some of these were, in retrospect, rash. But I was given the gift of self-confidence by my parents, and this sharpened a natural tilt toward the unknown. My wife and my children have also been essentially supportive of my interest in an unconventional career track and the risks attendant to that route. I have no tolerance for boredom and little for routine. Compensation arrangements have never been at the top of my list of professional priorities (at least not until the kids began arriving). I was always more interested in the challenge of the position and the excitement of the life to be lived.

Many of the good things that have happened to me professionally and many of the best friends I have made have come about through my participation in community service activities. Whether these have been bar associations or church activities, or others in service to my city or state, they have been critical to my sense of being part of a community effort directed to good ends, and they have led to unexpected professional opportunities. These activities are necessary and nourishing to a balanced life as a citizen.

Finally, I have been lucky to find people who would take a chance on me. At every important step of my professional journey, I have been guided directly or indirectly by someone whose friendship, interest in my well-being, and belief in what I could contribute has made the difference. Many times, this person did not appear until after I found myself in a new situation. Sometimes, his or her influence wasn't apparent to me until after I had left one situation and entered into another. But it seems to me now that there was always someone who has played this role: mentor, confidant, giver of courage.

My advice to young people about to enter upon their professional lives?

1. Make professional choices based on the quality of the people with whom you will be surrounded, not the financial terms or the prestige of the position.

2. Remember that what is important to you will change. Don't be frustrated by this—expect it and embrace it.

3. Look for ways to serve your profession and your community. This service will pay unexpected dividends in how you feel about yourself, your community, and what you can achieve.

4. Put yourself in the way of good luck. Understand what you love and find ways to pursue that interest, even if those ways are not immediately remunerative or conventional.

5. Always take a chance when you can. Never be discouraged by the odds or the amount of work. You were born to do great things. Get busy.

OUR OWN STORIES

We can speak to the advice offered here in part because of our own experiences in creating the work that we do and which we regard as our callings in life. Right out of college (where I, the elder Greene, majored in history), I entered law school with the intent of becoming either a lawyer or a college professor because of my strong interest in American history and particularly constitutional law and its significant role in the creation and sustaining of our democratic system. However, I found the approach to legal education and the goals and values of the more successful students very different from my own. My discomfort was such that I decided to turn to teaching history in a private school in my hometown. I was not very confident that I would be a good teacher, but I wanted to give it a try. Teaching, counseling, and coaching high school students took hold almost immediately and I recognized that I was on the right path, though I could not predict where it would ultimately take me.

An opportunity to return to graduate school for a degree in counseling on a teaching fellowship presented itself to me, and I had to make a difficult decision sooner than I was prepared to. I was receiving good reviews from the headmaster of my school, the head of the history department, and even a number of my students. I also received a good deal of pleasure in helping to build a winning hockey team. What would I gain by giving up this comfortable position to move into graduate school and assume a different teaching responsibility? I had to ask myself over and over again: What if I didn't like the course work and what if I was not as successful as I seemed to be at the secondary school level? I then worked through the worst scenario exercise. This helped me realize that at the end of the graduate program, I would have earned an advanced degree from a prestigious university in the field of counseling and educational theory, having been exposed to some of the leading teacher/scholars in the field, and I would have experience in overseeing a group of new teachers in the making.

Suddenly the choice seemed very obvious to me. Well into my studies a year and a half later, I was contacted by the Dean of the College at Princeton University regarding a position as an admissions officer and faculty adviser to undergraduates. This was at a time when many of the major universities were initiating active outreach to disadvantaged and female students across the nation. The serendipity of this opportunity still amazes me, these many years later. I had no connection to Princeton and had no thought of making college admissions my career. However, the opportunity to have real impact on helping many deserving students enter a leading university and working with them in a counseling relationship seemed so right to me. I made a list of my professional strengths, my core values, and my strongest interests and then reviewed where could I most effectively act on them. This is how I arrived at the next path in my own journey through life's labyrinth, one that in time took me in the direction of a rewarding, challenging calling in the fields of educational counseling and writing.

I had by now enough confidence in myself in terms of the professional training I had built, a further level of self-awareness as to what satisfied my needs and my personality style, and an instinctive feel for the timeliness in creating an entirely new career field in educational counseling and consulting. Looking in the rearview mirror, I can see how each turn in the path that I took was a logical one. But at the time, I had to work through many questions and overcome many doubts before taking each next step. My passion for the role education plays in individual lives and the community, my apparent skills as a personal counselor, and my desire or need to create my own enterprise combined to lead me to where I am today. Without question, my educational foundation in the liberal arts enabled me to take on each of the challenges as I moved through my personal labyrinth.

* * *

I (the younger Greene) came to this career as an independent educational counselor and consultant from a somewhat different direction. Passionate about international affairs, foreign policy, and intercultural dialogue, as well as writing, I had known going into my college education that I would combine these interests in some fashion. Along the way, I was fortunate to participate in experiences like an internship with the U.S. Information Agency and a study abroad program in Germany, which confirmed some instincts and challenged others. As I graduated college, I was fairly certain I wanted to work in some international capacity, and focused my sights on the U.S. Foreign Service. I passed the written exam and took the Graduate Record Examination to prepare for a back-up set of applications to international relations–oriented master's degree programs. Then, it was off to Colorado for a gap year after college, during which I would pursue my passions for music, rugby, and skiing, while preparing admissions applications and sitting for the Foreign Service oral exams.

I subsequently passed the orals, but with a score too low to be selected for that year's class of officers. I didn't gain admission to several selective master's programs back East, but meanwhile discovered the public policy program at the University of Colorado right in my backyard. As I got to know the professors, graduate students, and administrators of the program, I realized I was already in the right place. I passed up a second opportunity to focus on foreign service and instead immersed myself in policy.

I began my journey into learning about schools at an early age, following my father's comments about the variety of schools with which he interacted as a consultant and counselor. My own education at public school through sixth grade and then at Hopkins, a challenging and diverse independent day school, taught me the importance of teachers, of peers, and of talented and caring administrators. Through college my interests in history, government, international relations, languages, and values shaped my approach to the world. I became strongly interested in cultures and institutions, and how they changed over time and contrasted with one another. As a graduate student with long-standing interests in conflict resolution and policy making, I began gradually to link my study of theories of nonviolence, such as those of Gandhi, King, and Gene Sharp, with my fascination for politics, policy making, and education. I became convinced that education was the primary way that we as a society could foster positive changes in values among our children. I joined the spheres of education policy and peace studies by researching peer mediation and school conflict resolution programs. I began volunteering as a community mediator and enjoyed the intense one-on-one counseling role I played there, as well as in my work as a teaching assistant and graduate teacher trainer at the university.

What I learned very quickly was that teaching students nonviolent methods for solving their problems was just the tip of the school violence iceberg. "The Problem," as such, was much more complicated and intricate than was suggested by the media, educators, and many academic scholars. While I had begun my inquiry with an earnest goal of supporting the development of positive, practical means of problem solving for youth, I opened a Pandora's box of value disagreements, education policy dilemmas, and fear and concern on the part of educators, parents, and students. My focus on school violence led me to a broader examination of the ways in which schools, as institutions, define and learn about any problem or issue they face.

After six years of intense work, I graduated not only with my master's degree but also with my Ph.D. in political science. I had crafted my degree to focus on educational policy making and done everything I could to zero in on schools and students as the core of my inquiry. Surprise hit me one day in talking with my father when I realized that a career in our family business would allow me to research, write, counsel students, and enjoy my hobbies and independence. Thirteen years of educational counseling, consulting, research, and writing, working with a diverse group of students, families, secondary schools, and colleges have allowed me to compare and reflect on the ways in which different students and different institutions learn. I make a difference every day with individual students, through my writing and in my community. I am using my college and graduate educational skills constantly, though not necessarily in the way I had intended.

6

THE ART OF REFLECTING ON YOUR EXPERIENCES

> Reflection is the business of man; a sense of his state is his first duty: but who remembereth himself in joy? Is it not in mercy then that sorrow is allotted unto us?
>
> —WILLIAM SHAKESPEARE

EVERY EXPERIENCE YOU HAVE IS an opportunity to learn. Try to learn from every experience. To do this, you need to reflect on your experiences and draw lessons from them. You can learn from both success and failure, and that learning can positively impact your future choices. Reflection is the process of considering what has transpired in your life and seeking conclusions and meaning that will affect your future decision making.

LESSON DRAWING

The idea of drawing lessons from your experiences is not a new one. Yet many of us do not sit back on a regular basis and say to ourselves, "What should I learn from this event? Are there any lessons here for me which I should remember for the future?" You don't need to practice Zen meditation to reflect on your experiences and draw lessons from them (though you could). You could also write in a journal; talk to a trusted friend, parent, or mentor; or read books and articles that comment on what you have just gone through.

At its simplest level, lesson drawing can consist of making a list of possible conclusions you could make given what has occurred. Let's say, for example, that you have just completed what you thought was a successful internship at a large company. This company is known to hire a large percentage of its new employees through the internship program, and to make offers to most of those interns each year, provided that they were reasonably well received during the course of the internship. You had a good relationship with your supervisor, completed several projects, and felt that you knew what you were doing. Yet at the conclusion of your program, you were overlooked for a job offer and had to return to your last year of college empty-handed. What happened?

In talking with students we have counseled, we have often found that they tend to draw the wrong lessons from such experiences, or overreact in ways that could seriously impact their future choices. Some might list several lessons from this experience that go way off track or are too personally negative. For example:

- Nobody likes me, and I just don't know how to succeed in an office environment (yes, we've heard this!).

- I just don't understand the banking/advertising/ trading/sales industry and what they want.

- My courses and grades are not good enough to get this kind of a job.

- Maybe this is the wrong career for me.

You need to think beyond the most simplistic conclusions if you are to draw real and valuable lessons from an experience like this. Perhaps you aren't good at this particular kind of job, but if you enjoyed what you were doing and felt successful, then that doesn't sound right. To confirm or dispel this notion, you need to talk with your supervisor and consider the reviews you received during and after your internship to see what the problems were, if any, with your performance. It may be that, during this hiring cycle, there just weren't as many entry-level jobs available for people with your skill set, or the company is selling a division, or is preparing to offer itself up for sale. The lesson could be that you must seek to learn more about the larger environment shaping the company you are working for and industry you are working in. In addition to focusing on your own job and performance, you need to be aware of what is happening politically, institutionally, and culturally in an organization.

If you were offered an internship, it is likely that the company found enough worthwhile in your college performance and initial interview or application to offer you an opportunity. It is unlikely that they subsequently didn't offer you a job based on your college transcript. It is more likely that, in addition to the impersonal forces noted above which could have been working against you, the company found something lacking in your actual performance of your duties. Perhaps you didn't fully understand what those duties were, or didn't act proactively enough to seek out new challenges and opportunities. The lesson could be that once you have an opportunity like this in hand, you need to be as energetic as possible in finding ways to help your supervisor and employer. Perhaps you need to be more explicit in asking for direction in your work, and make sure to regularly communicate with your boss to see that you are performing as they expect. Another lesson? Never assume anything about job offers until a contract is in your hand, and never count bonus checks until the funds are in your bank account.

We have seen many examples of students "over-drawing" lessons, which they later regret. For example, there was the young woman who always wanted to be a doctor but who encountered a terrible freshman biology class and instructor at a large university. She failed the introductory class, which was graded on a forced curve, and never took a science again because she "just wasn't smart enough to succeed in college-level biology." Yet now, five years later, having graduated from college without finding a calling that motivated her, she still thought wistfully about helping people through medicine and wondered whether there was still time to become a doctor. There was, through enrolling in a post-baccalaureate premedical program.

Other lessons she could have drawn from her failure in freshman biology? I don't do well in large lecture classes and should stick to smaller, discussion-oriented courses. Perhaps I'm in the wrong college. Or, I need to make sure I pick classes where the professor is better; and if I end up with a bad instructor, I need to drop the course and take it again later.

To draw accurate lessons from your experiences, we encourage you to delve more deeply—to second-, third-, and fourth-level conclusions; to possibilities you might not have considered, opinions that differ from your own. Sometimes the simplest and most obvious answer is the right one. Other times, the situation is much more complicated. And remember your Thread. If you are still focused on the passions that compel you to move forward, then don't let an instance of failure deter you, or an easy success lull you into complacency.

SEEING FAILURES AS LEARNING OPPORTUNITIES

Ask yourself why you have failed in an attempt, and you might be able to avoid future disappointments. That is not to say that failures should be viewed only as minor setbacks as you continue on your way toward the same goal. A failure can change that goal, or shape it in surprising ways.

Sometimes a failure is a chance to step back and be released from a constraining career or educational path. If you have been working to fulfill someone else's vision for your future (often a parent's), then trying that path and either finding it not to your liking or getting real negative feedback can take the burden of that commitment from you. It will no longer be your responsibility to reach that goal.

A failure can very much be a wake-up call as well. Listen for lessons as to why you failed, in your head, heart, and gut. You will know if you didn't work hard enough; if you were not qualified; if you were a fish out of water. Perhaps you will need to work harder, become more dedicated, or get further training if you want to make it next time.

SEEING SUCCESSES AS LEARNING OPPORTUNITIES

Easy success, academically or professionally, does not often produce as much reflection and learning as a hard-won accomplishment or a failure. If you are doing well, you should be just as aware of the need to reflect on why you have been succeeding. And you should watch out for pitfalls and blindspots associated with overconfidence or a lack of self-awareness.

We are reminded of the young man we counseled to medical school who had always been told that medicine was the best way for him to work with young people, as a pediatrician. Not only did he graduate from an Ivy League university, but he also gained admission to medical school on his first attempt. He was well on his way toward becoming a physician when he realized he was on the wrong track. Halfway through his program, he realized that what he really enjoyed was teaching students independently, and he dropped out of medical school to found his own very successful tutoring business.

Had he not stopped in the midst of his success to reflect on his lack of contentment with his journey, he would likely have woken up some years from now just as dissatisfied with his continued involvement in a field that was okay for him, but not exciting.

Just as important is stopping to consider the work you have put in to get where you are, and the people who helped you make it there. You probably have some work to do to thank those who supported you financially and emotionally, who mentored you and taught you, who sacrificed as you succeeded. We are reminded of a speech Fred Rogers, creator of *Mr. Rogers' Neighborhood,* gave at the Dartmouth College commencement in 2002, repeating one of his favorite themes:

> I'D LIKE TO GIVE YOU all an invisible gift. A gift of a silent minute to think about those who have helped you become who you are today. Some of them may be here right now. Some may be far away. Some . . . may even be in Heaven. But wherever they are, if they've loved you and encouraged you and wanted what was best in life for you, they're right inside yourself. And I feel that you deserve quiet time on this special occasion to devote some thought to them. So let's just take a minute in honor of those who have cared about us all along the way. One silent minute.
>
> Whomever you've been thinking about, imagine how grateful they must be that during your silent times you remember how important they are to you. It's not the honors and the prizes and the fancy outsides of life which ultimately nourish our souls. It's the knowing that we can be trusted, that we never have to fear the truth, that the bedrock of our lives from which we make our choices is very good stuff.

As you succeed and fail along your path in life, take those silent minutes to reflect on what has worked for you, and what hasn't, and do your best to draw the right lessons from your experiences.

FRAMING YOUR NARRATIVE

Framing involves how you portray the narrative of what has happened, is happening, and will happen to you. One can re-frame events, turning "negative" things like layoffs into "positive" things like an opportunity to switch gears, go back to school, and learn some lessons. What is your narrative? What is the Thread that ties your experiences together? How has your choice of major affected your college performance, and what does that suggest for future graduate degrees or jobs? Why weren't you chosen for that analyst training track? Why weren't you accepted to the graduate programs you applied to? What can you learn from the feedback you receive from your supervisors, and how can you reframe your understanding of that information to make sense of it?

As you learn from successes and failures and continue to define who you are and where you see yourself going, you will have choices in terms of how you frame your story. You can think of your frame as the light in which you cast an event. The frame is how you spin the story. What is your evolving answer to these questions?

- What do you do?

- What brought you here?

- How did you end up in this job (or college, or internship)?

- What do you want to be (or do with your life) when you grow up?

Be prepared to answer these questions to yourself, to your friends, to your folks, and to current and prospective employers, teachers, and new network connections. How? One hint is to keep searching for your Threads.

WRITING YOUR STORY

Most of you will have taken an expository or creative writing class. Or had an interview for college or a job. Or sat down for dinner with friends of your parents, business associates, or new classmates. As you are asked the kinds of questions listed above, you need to start somewhere. You might have a clear, declarative "I am a ———." beginning. This can help you define yourself and the rest will follow. Of course, if you're reading this book, odds are that you're still seeking the solution to filling in the blank at the end of that sentence. So let's backtrack a bit.

Where did you start? What is your beginning? You can begin at the beginning, with where you were born, but unless that is particularly relevant to how you frame your story, then you might gloss over the early years and jump to that which is most connected to the Thread you have been following for some time. You have made decisions during the past ten, twenty, or more years. You might have chosen where to live, where to go to high school, where to go to college, what to major in, what not to major in, whether to take part in an exchange or internship or study abroad program, which activities to participate in, and where to work, live, and raise a family. What is most of interest to the listener or reader is *why*.

Why did you make the decisions you did? What ties them together? How can you explain events of your choosing, and frame situations beyond your control? These might include the loss of a parent, an illness, being laid off from a job, or being moved around the country or the world by parents involved in the armed forces or international businesses. How did you react to events that happened to you, and what did you learn? How did you choose to achieve other outcomes? What values have been important in your narrative?

The interesting thing about frames is that they can shift over time, and that your story is still in progress. You will likely find yourself reshaping your frame as you grow and learn. What you wanted to do when you entered college is likely not what you are doing now. You don't need to erase your earlier preferences, but you can now note what you had thought you would do and then draw the connections to how you ended up where you are now. Here is one example: "I thought I was going to study business, but I took my first class in finance and found it uninteresting. Meanwhile, my art history teacher was fascinating and I chose to study in Rome during my junior year. I was hooked. I still like business and am good with numbers, and that is why I'm now thinking of pursuing a career with an international auction house."

THE PRESIDENT OF JUILLIARD WRITES HIS STORY

Joseph Polisi is an accomplished educator now serving as President of The Juilliard School in New York City. As he makes clear in framing his own narrative, his path to his current career followed some very clear Threads and enabled him to combine his passions in a unique way.

IN THINKING OF MY CAREER in arts education, which now spans over 30 years, the one thread that constantly surfaces is my love of music. I grew up as a bassoonist and the son of the principal bassoon of the New York Philharmonic (William Polisi). My mother was a dancer, so the arts were very much a part of our family.

I decided at a young age to become a lawyer, but I also became a capable bassoonist. When I was a senior in high school, I asked my dad if I should apply to Juilliard (where he taught) or to Curtis (from which he graduated). He asked a great question of me: Is music the only thing you want to do in your life? I responded that I didn't know and he quickly said that those two schools were not yet for me.

I enrolled at the University of Connecticut as a political science major and deferred going to law school upon the recommendation of my adviser, who was a graduate of the Fletcher School of Law and Diplomacy. I entered Fletcher and earned a M.A. in International Relations, but I felt like a fish out of water. I felt no passion for what I was doing. The Vietnam War was raging at the time and the term *relevancy* was quite prevalent. For me the term meant, how is your profession going to make you and the world better? International banking or the law no longer seemed to be my destination. Now I was ready for music school and enrolled as a graduate student at the Yale School of Music.

I remember asking myself, what is the skill set I possess that presents my greatest talents? I had always excelled at music and I was naturally drawn to that profession, whatever that turned out to be. Now I help run one of the great arts education schools in the world. My graduate studies in music have meshed perfectly with my earlier studies in political science and international relations. (I often see more bankers, lawyers, investors, and foreign service officers in a day than I do artists!)

The moral of my story is that I followed my passion and evaluated what my best talents were. My position as President of Juilliard requires of me the many skills found in the subjects I studied in college and graduate school, but I would never have predicted that I would use them as I do every day at Juilliard.

TURNING PAST AND PRESENT INTO FUTURE

As you have framed your past you can put yourself in your present and continue to forecast your future. We now move to a discussion of some of the ways in which you can plan your next steps, from short-term progress to long-term goal-setting. We discuss attaining a graduate degree, as well as balancing money and material needs with your sense of values and their importance to you in your work life.

7

THE MAGIC OF UNPLANNED OPPORTUNITIES

> Serendipity. Look for something, find something else, and realize that what you've found is more suited to your needs than what you thought you were looking for.
>
> —LAWRENCE BLOCK, NOVELIST

LIFE IS FULL OF UNPLANNED and random opportunities and encounters. Learning to take advantage of happenstance and seizing the moment can be crucial to finding your way. Things don't always go according to plan. What is important is to assess whether you have followed your Thread into a new opportunity, or whether you have arrived at a cul de sac.

TAKING ADVANTAGE OF SURPRISES

While you go about all that planning for your future, be open to chance interactions and offers that might allow you to find your direction. Such unlooked for discoveries may just turn out to be defining events. Opportunities you didn't know existed. *Aha*! moments that provide you with clarity where before there was confusion.

How do you prepare for events that are by definition unsought and unprepared for? As Louis Pasteur noted, "In the field of observation, chance favors only the prepared mind." That is, if you have been doing the reflective work to know yourself and consider your life's Thread or Threads, then you are more likely recognize a good (and appropriate) opportunity when you see one.

Tricia's story in our Introduction to this book illustrates well the ways in which serendipity, but in a sense, logical chance, can impact your career development. As we will see, being open to the powers of serendipity will require you to balance your tolerance of risk, your values, and your willingness to reinvent yourself. For Tricia, it took a car accident to bring her home and on to a job at a major organization. Though her passion was international education, Tricia did not give up the chance to work at the College Board. She then took advantage of that opportunity she had there to travel across the United States and built upon her interests and skills. From there, she has continued to follow her Thread, and has brought her interest in international studies back into her work.

Another way to look at the concept of serendipity is to consider whether you are wearing blinders right now. Are you so focused on attaining one ultimate goal that you are ignoring other interesting possibilities that might be passing you by? Are you looking so straight ahead that you cannot see slightly to the left or right of you? If so, then you might be missing out, as Robert Frost put it, on some road "less traveled by." You will need to set goals in your career planning, but keeping your mind prepared for chance discoveries can be crucial for your development and satisfaction.

MYOPIC CAREER DEVELOPMENT

Sometimes career planning is the art of proceeding from one successful experience to the next in a short-term, focused procession. If you like something a lot, do more of it. If you continue to like it, keep doing it. If something opens up that is highly attractive, take advantage of it. Before long, you might have found a vocation and created a career. To use this approach, you have to focus on what you are doing, and how you can follow that Thread from one step to another.

We find that career planning is typically a bouncing back and forth between myopia and longer-term goal setting. Having a vision for your future—of you in one year, five years, ten years, twenty years—can help you work backward to the steps you need to take to get there, all the while focusing on and being conscious of current successes, failures, and tangents. Your long-term vision will evolve as you reflect on your short-term experiences.

LIVING LIFE ON THE CHESSBOARD (OR THE WRESTLING MAT)

If you play chess, you are familiar with the notion of an evolving game, one in which you have both shifting long-term strategies and immediate challenges you must respond to. At times you might be thinking only one or two moves ahead, even as you forecast a variety of scenarios that could play out to your benefit or demise in five or ten or more moves. Your opponent is simultaneously countering and planning and shifting. Now, in life we might not have an opponent consistently trying to beat us at our own game (at least we hope not), but we do have shifting circumstances to which we must respond. We must adapt when put in a surprise *check,* and make sure we survive an imminent danger. Meanwhile, we look forward to see how we can turn the situation to our benefit.

Judo and wrestling offer other metaphors to illustrate this point. One has a plan of attack, a game plan for the match. Yet one must also react to an opponent's moves, using their weight and momentum to turn the match to your advantage. As you roll with it, so to speak, you must assess the situation. What is working? What is not? What difficulties are you encountering which require new approaches, new ideas? Do you need to rethink your initial plan? Perhaps your usual leg holds are not working against this challenger. Are you in the wrong arena altogether?

Without trying to stretch these metaphors too far, we want you to see the need for you to think on your feet. Move your field of focus back and forth between long-term planning and short-term needs. This requires ongoing lesson drawing and an open-minded willingness to reframe your story, learning from successes and failures. You won't put an opponent into checkmate unless you are thinking several moves ahead and comparing a current strategic situation to your knowledge of past games played or read about. Yet if you are so focused on pursuing one particular checkmate strategy and are unwilling to shift your plan in the face of immediate setbacks, then you run the risk of losing the game.

DOES THIS MEAN IT'S OKAY TO BE SHORTSIGHTED?

Yes. Becoming consciously shortsighted can help you live more in the present and to seek meaning from each experience you are having while you are having it. If you don't look in your immediate life's mirror, you might miss something. Something important. If you are really good at a job and are finding success, why should you change a good thing? Isn't is okay to sit back and say to yourself, "Hey, I'm pretty good at this. Maybe this is my calling. . . ."? This will force you to be honest with yourself about why you feel a need to change tracks when you are finding current success.

Perhaps you're not making enough money? Maybe you can brew as good a latte as the best barista, and might make manager someday, but you're not going to establish the material standard of living you had in mind that way.

Perhaps you're not finding enough meaning in your work? Coffee gets people through their day, to be sure, but are you really changing the world and doing enough good with your life?

Perhaps you're not finding enough intellectual stimulation? There's a great crowd at the café, and some cool used books on the shelves, but those thirty-second conversations about Hegel while you get a pastry just aren't satisfying your need for mental aerobics. "Why did I go to college?" you might be wondering.

On the other hand, we have worked with many individuals who have found themselves doing well in an area they never imagined would become their career. Consider the recent graduate who began a teaching internship at a middle school after college as a way to do something while planning a real career. He confided to us that he loved his job, stressful as it was, and felt he was really making a difference in the lives of his students. What's more, he knew he was good at it. The problem? His parents, and perhaps the wider culture, had instilled in him the notion that teaching wasn't good enough for him. It was fine for some people, but it wasn't prestigious, glamorous, or remunerative enough to satisfy his needs. Yet as he looked at the short-term view, this young man was able to see that the needs he wasn't trying to satisfy didn't belong to him at all.

Elliot L. Richardson, a graduate of Harvard Law School, had a highly successful career serving as U.S. attorney for Massachusetts, attorney general for Massachusetts, Secretary of Health, Education and Welfare, Secretary of Defense, Attorney General of the United States, Secretary of Commerce, and ambassador to Great Britain. He also clerked for two U.S. Supreme Court justices, Felix Frankfurter and Learned Hand. He is quoted as describing this advice he received, which we believe is very much in the spirit of celebrating a certain amount of myopia in your life.

ALTHOUGH THEY WERE GREAT FRIENDS, Frankfurter and Hand could not have been more different. Learned Hand immersed himself in his work and had very little activity outside the law. It was almost the other way around with Frankfurter. He had lots of visitors and he was reading all the time—books on philosophy, books on policy, books on comparative literature. I can't now remember what brought it up, but one day Frankfurter said to me, "Elliot, I don't think you ought to develop career goals. I've known quite a few men who did this, and then they did everything in their power to fulfill this ambition. They were constantly calculating how to take advantage of some opportunity or connection that would move them along toward their goal. Yet, most of them awaken in their fifties to the realization that they are never going to achieve their great ambition. On top of that disappointment, they realize that they undercut the satisfaction of what they were doing by trying to use it for the sake of something else." I thought that was very insightful advice, and I took it to heart. Each job, each case, carries its own reward, and beyond that there are no worthwhile rewards. The reward is in doing the job well, in doing the best you can, and in the belief that it was useful.

So focus on your current job or pursuit. Do it well, and then consider your next logical step. Good results will follow.

8

DELAYING GRATIFICATION AND BUILDING YOUR CREDENTIALS

> Endurance is the crowning quality,
> And patience all the passion of great hearts.
>
> —JAMES RUSSELL LOWELL

A CARTOON THAT APPEARED IN the *New Yorker* shows a young man who is interviewing with an employment consultant and explaining what his goals are: "I'm looking for a position where I can slowly lose sight of what I originally set out to do with my life, with benefits."

Success in finding your eventual calling requires a focus on the long term with continual reviews of where you are at a particular point in your life and how you got there, and what could or should be the next stages of building toward your eventual goal. Which still may present a hazy view of your future. You have lots of important decisions to make in the early phase after college:

- Do I remain in a position that is not terribly interesting or exciting or move on to another?

- How long do I need to remain in my present situation in order to build a respectable résumé?

- Is this the right time to make a move?

- Am I learning a lot for myself from my present work?

- Should I go to graduate school at this point or do I even need an advanced degree or formal certification for what I want to do with my life?

- Do I want to give up my present income or relative freedom to undergo the demands of further studies?

- How willing am I to take on debt to pay for another degree or certificate program?

- Should I take a break from what I am doing and just travel and explore new fields of interest?

- Should I leave my graduate studies because I think I chose the wrong program?

Earlier we described the traits of persistence and the ability to delay pleasurable activities while in college which enabled you to meet all of your academic and organizational obligations and earn your diploma. These traits are critical to you now that you are out in a larger environment where you need to prove to yourself and to others that you are committed to your job or internship and will see any assignments through to completion. You also need time and experience to be clear about what your eventual goals are, and whether you need advanced educational training and a formal degree that is both relevant and helpful in meeting your goals.

It may become obvious early on that graduate training is either required or essential in a great number of fields, the most obvious being medicine and health care, the law, education at all levels, the ministry, science and technology, and increasingly, business management and finance. Growing numbers of college graduates are applying to all of the professional graduate programs related to these fields. The key concern for you is to discover which one of these professions, among many others, fit with your goals and when is the best time for you to enroll.

Joseph Polisi, Juilliard's president, had the following opinions about when a student should pursue graduate studies.

> I HAVE ADVISED GRADUATING SENIORS to follow their passion regarding which field to pursue in the future. Often a "passion" for a field is manifested by a natural ability in that field and an ease and comfort in dealing with the challenges of that profession, whether it be in finance or music. I'm often asked by recent graduates if they should pursue further study, in particular doctoral work. My response is

that advanced study should be pursued only if the individual has a strong desire to delve deeper into a specific discipline. Pursuing a doctorate only to receive a credential to improve chances of obtaining a job neither serves the individual or the profession well.

QUESTIONS TO ASK YOURSELF BEFORE GOING TO GRADUATE SCHOOL

There are a number of very basic questions to raise when considering enrolling in graduate school:

- Have I had sufficient career or academic exposure to make a commitment to graduate education in a particular field?

- Is a professional graduate degree required in the field I am aiming for? If so, what kind of training do I need and what are the most appropriate and realistic options for me?

- Do I understand that graduate school education in all fields is highly focused on training for specific professional roles? (The assumption of the faculty is that a student knows what his or her goals are and wants a structured curriculum to prepare him or her accordingly.)

- Am I prepared to apply to graduate programs in terms of my college field of study, grade-point average, and required admissions testing? Do I have enough experience in the particular field to qualify and to impress an admissions committee?

- Can I afford to leave my present position financially and will I be able to cover the tuition through savings, loans, assistance from my family or employer, or grants and scholarships?

- Am I psychologically and emotionally prepared to return to formal academic studies?

- Am I flexible in terms of where I would consider living and how I would handle personal relationships while pursuing graduate studies?

- Am I willing to attend a graduate school program that is not considered to be one of the top-rated, or am I too concerned with the prestige factor?

- Am I considering graduate school for the right reasons? Am I just using it as an acceptable way of leaving an uninteresting position or because I am confused about what I want to do with my life?

- Would I be better served by taking certification courses in a specialized field at a local university or online?

- Do I have more to gain by remaining in my current position and learning as much as I can before I make a next move? Will I lose the opportunity to grow more by this practical experience and exposure to people in the field?

- Am I jumping into a popular career track more because there are lots of job opportunities at this time and less because my genuine interests have led me to it?

It should be evident from the above that your acquired skills in analyzing circumstances and choices, weighing the benefits and lost opportunity costs associated with graduate studies, researching how and where to apply to any graduate program, and delaying jumping before you are ready should come into play in considering advanced studies. One fact is very clear: You should by this stage recognize the importance of continually learning on your own. Reading any and every book or article related to your field is a must. Talking as often as is reasonable with your supervisor will teach you a great deal. It is possible that you are better served at this time by sticking with what you are doing and working your way into positions of greater responsibility and leadership than in leaving too soon for graduate school.

We recall a young man who had majored in business at a competitive college and then found a series of jobs prior to landing a good sales position at a major health-care products

MANY LIBERAL ARTS GRADUATES DELAY ENTRANCE TO GRADUATE SCHOOL IN A VARIETY OF FIELDS

According to Skip Sturman, Director of the Career Services office at Dartmouth College, typically 20 to 25 percent of Dartmouth graduating seniors go directly to graduate school each year. A recent survey of graduates one year out of Dartmouth showed that of the 21 percent enrolled full-time in graduate programs, 17 percent were in medical school and 23 percent in law school. Those surveyed who were not in graduate school identified a wide range of career fields as their full-time employment. These included: consulting (16 percent), financial services (15 percent), education (12 percent), the nonprofits sector (6 percent), government (5 percent), and health care (4 percent).

company. He was intent on pursuing graduate studies in business, which he felt were essential for his career advancement. He would not be an obvious admit at the top business schools since he had a good GPA but was not at a top 10 percent standing or have a high GMAT score. He also had only a few years of work experience, rather than the four to six years most top business schools are looking for nowadays.

When we began working with him, we explained the tension between staying put and getting more experience in his current company versus trying to move quickly into graduate studies. During the course of three years' work, during which he did not move into business school, we watched him gradually move up the ladder in his company. Even as he prepared graduate applications, he was offered positions of increasing responsibility and in-house training opportunities in sales, marketing, and management. Additionally, he continued to make contacts among the clients he worked with and the venture capital community in San Francisco, where he was based. What became increasingly obvious was that he did not need an MBA, at least at this point in his life, and perhaps never. His learning curve was challenging and his advancement productive. He just needed to focus more on the present and less on the assumed need for a graduate degree when his career was already happening.

IDENTIFYING THE RIGHT KIND OF WORK ENVIRONMENT FOR YOURSELF

Albert Einstein said that imagination is more important than knowledge. Of course, both are essential for creating an exciting, meaningful life's work. Standing back from your immediate situation and reviewing the dreams you have developed and want to fulfill should come first. Remind yourself every so often, especially when you have those moments of doubt about why you are doing what you are, that finding your calling is a process that takes time and patience to develop. It is not a straight line from A to Z in terms of real experiences and advanced education.

Every leader we have talked with expressed his concern about too much jumping around from one brief period of work to the next when reviewing potential employees. This is especially a concern when there does not appear to be a logical or understandable common thread to the many different experiences. Keep this in mind before you allow your impatience to lead you to make a move that does not represent an appropriate opportunity for experience, learning, and leadership.

Whether you are about to graduate from college or are in the early stages of a postcollege experience, there are some important questions to consider at this time before you make any commitments. With each situation you take on you will be better able to determine your preferences in each of these categories. You will also gain a clearer picture of whether you need graduate school training at some point:

- What kind of organizational environment appeals to me the most? Do I prefer to work in a highly structured corporate setting or one that is small, intimate, and more flexible?

- Do I prefer to work with others in a hierarchical or team-oriented setting, or do I prefer to work on my own and for myself?

- How much do I care about attaining a great deal of money and prestige?

- Do I prefer to work in a for-profit or nonprofit organization?

- How much importance do I attach to an organization's culture and thus its values and goals? Do I prefer
  a financial bottom-line orientation or an orientation
  to serve the community?

- Do I want the security of a well-established organization that has a successful history or do I want to
  participate in a young or a startup enterprise that I can
  help to build?

- How do I feel about the particular expectations of the
  working environment? Do I do well in situations where
  explicit goals are set by others and are expected to be
  met, with success or failure thus defined by numbers?
  Or do I function better in a more relaxed setting where
  I will set my own goals within the organization's
  mission and create ways to accomplish them?

- How important is a work schedule? Do I like a fixed
  nine-to-five type of position, a 24/7 culture that
  expects me to be working under pressure and on
  demand, or do I want a more flexible schedule that lets
  me choose how and when I will complete my responsibilities?

- Do I care strongly about where I live and work? Am I
  an urbanite who cannot enjoy life without being in a

large city, or do I feel more at home in a suburban or small town or rural setting?

- What kinds of people do I want as my colleagues? Does it matter to me or is it important to be engaged with individuals who share my values, interests, and background? Do I need an intellectually challenging environment?

- Do I want coworkers at all? Or am I more content and productive by working on my own projects or profession?

- Do I see myself in a highly professional role that requires a high level of educational training and expertise?

- Do I want travel on a regular basis to be a required part of my work? Do I want to experience new settings and interact with different cultures?

- How important is having a family to me, and how will I balance my family and work life?

The capacity to think through these issues as you follow your Thread through the labyrinth will enable you to gain further and deeper insights into your personal priorities. You will become more confident about your next steps toward your calling. You will be better positioned to decide whether to stay on in a particular position or change to another, or if it is appropriate to enter an advanced degree program.

THE VITAL IMPORTANCE OF FINDING GOOD MENTORS

The leaders in a variety of enterprises whom we interviewed all commented on the role a talented, caring mentor played in their professional lives. We recently heard a professor at the Wharton School of Business at the University of Pennsylvania who teaches courses in leadership discuss the significant influence that mentors had in guiding promising employees in their charge through the complexities of their organizations.

To find a mentor, try to identify one or more persons in your college or work organization whom you respect and trust intuitively. A mentor should be able to explain the culture of the organization and what skills and experiences are most important to develop. A mentor should be able to counsel you as to whether further formal education is either required or recommended. Listen to the counsel of such a person carefully. You may find that your instinct or urge to change your job or to apply to graduate school is premature. There might still be much to gain from your present exposure and patience might be called for. A trusted mentor can prove of great value to you at this juncture.

John Wooden, the legendary basketball coach at UCLA who won an unprecedented number of national championships and influenced the lives of hundreds of outstanding athletes he coached, put our thought here directly and succinctly: "It's what you learn after you know it all that counts." Catch the irony in his counsel. There is a tendency to think you have learned everything you need to know from your early experiences in a field and thus to jump to the next job or to believe you are now ready to earn a graduate degree that will take you to new heights of responsibility, leadership, and income. Do your research on what skills and education are necessary or advantageous for success in your chosen field, talk to your mentors about your preparedness, and then study the programs to find the one that would suit you the best.

Be mindful that taking your time in any paid or volunteer position to demonstrate your abilities and to build a network of contacts will pay off handsomely in the longer run. This may help you stay committed to your work and delay that impulse to leap into a new situation, be it another position or graduate school, too soon. You should focus your energies on identifying roles where you can satisfy the needs of a for-profit, a community service, a nonprofit, or a governmental organization that aligns with your skills. If you land such a position, take as long as necessary to prove your value while learning more about the work and honing your skill sets. Do not be impatient because you are at the lower end of the ladder initially. Patience, persistence, consistency, learning by doing, and finding a quality role model will all be re-warded in time.

WHY (AND WHEN AND HOW) YOU SHOULD CONSIDER ADVANCED EDUCATION

The economic prognosticators within the government, fi-nancial, and university worlds agree that the fastest growing occupations in the foreseeable future will be in the profes-sions of health care, law, education, technology and science, engineering, computer and information science, executive leadership, and management in all public and private organi-zations. The requirements for higher levels of expertise will continue to increase, thus putting a higher premium on ad-vanced levels of education. You are very likely to need to en-roll in graduate studies at some point in your early career. There are advantages to having advanced-level training in most fields today. The key consideration is to be convinced that you have found the field that excites you and to which you have had enough exposure to make the right choice of graduate training.

It should be pretty clear at this point that opting to enroll in graduate school must be a very considered decision. Many undergraduates continue to apply directly from college to graduate programs for one or a combination of several rea-sons, all of which can lead to disappointment and a sense of failure. The first reason is a certainty about a career goal framed as a vague concept, such as, "I always wanted to be a doctor and care for people," or "I have always thought it would be cool to be a lawyer and work as prosecutor in a district attorney's office." These are only two of hundreds of examples we could mention.

The second reason students apply too early to graduate school is the very opposite kind of thinking that can also motivate graduating seniors: I have no idea of what I want to do with my life, so if I go to graduate school I will discover what it is I want to do. Liberal arts graduates are particularly vulnerable to the siren call of law school or business school because they know that these graduate schools encourage liberal arts majors to apply. How often do we hear students say to us, "I know that I can really do anything I want in the future with a law degree or a business degree"?

A third reason why many apply directly to graduate school is their sense that you have better odds of acceptance to premier programs as a recent grad than if you are out of college and have been out in the world for a while. This assumption is false.

Reason four is tied to parental expectations that result in the pressure to continue studies in graduate school. Parents' reasons are most often emotional, we find. Parents are concerned that if their son or daughter does not go directly to graduate school, he or she will get sidetracked out in the world and will never return to formal studies for a professional career.

If any or all of these premises apply to you, you could be headed down the wrong path in the labyrinth. Let's explain why:

REASON ONE: Unless you have used your time in college to get up close to the profession that you are considering by any of the ways we have described earlier, you may be fooling yourself as to what is required in terms of aptitudes, qualifications, and personality. Before you jump into the application process, engage in key activities of interning, volunteering, researching, shadowing a practitioner in the field as well as visiting several graduate schools to learn about the curricular requirements and the typical profile of enrolled students.

REASON TWO: Graduate schools in every field take it as an assumption that a student is there to develop the knowledge base and particular skills to become a highly successful professional in time. Therefore, the required courses and out of class programs have been designed to lead to this end. Professional graduate school is not an environment that encourages wide-ranging exploration or a cafeteria selection of courses in order to find yourself. You want to be as certain as you can early on because of your exposure that you are on the right training ground and have a pretty good idea of the field in which you will want to pursue your calling.

REASON THREE: It naturally follows that a graduate school faculty puts a very high premium on related experiences and a focused student in their classrooms. They want to teach and mentor individuals who have had experience dealing with the core demands and issues in the field of their expertise. The classroom ethos is one of active, often aggressive student give and take. Having confidence in oneself based on some level of experience in the field becomes essential to survival and success. Ask any recent graduate of any professional school.

REASON FOUR: Taking on the demands and pressure of a graduate program in which the major driver is someone other than yourself can be a terrible experience. If you do not have a high level of interest in the subject matter and a vision of a fulfilling future in the particular field, you could be miserable. Before you make this kind of commitment, talk through with your family why you already know that you lack the interest and motivation to pursue such studies, or that you need more exposure through field experience and research to be convinced this is the right direction for you.

The following letter from an active colleague with whom we have had the pleasure of working on several PBS television specials can be read as a strong case for gaining maturity and insight into your strengths and some of the essential ingredients that lead to ultimate reward in any chosen calling. Delayed gratification is a lesson implicit in this story. The writer is a highly experienced consultant in the Internet and public television fields.

DEAR HOWARD AND MATTHEW:

My latest "boss" on a project is a twenty-year-old from an Ivy League university. He and three classmates are developing a very interesting Web application to encourage electronic democracy. I thought you would be interested in hearing my tales.

The three have a hefty investor and I have been hired by the investor's people to keep them on track. That's a laugh, I have discovered. To say they are young, cocky, and inexperienced is a gross understatement. They are very talented, and I guess the attitudes come with the territory. It has been both fun and a major challenge working with them, and I hope I have taught them a bit about the necessity of teamwork, communication, follow through, and the setting of high standards. The truth is that most of what I say is disregarded, and they do what they want. All I can do is model the process of professionalism and hope that some of this will rub off on them.

I believe that these young men and this project would have benefitted greatly if they possessed BOTH talent and basic business skills. The one who is the boss is mean. He thinks being a boss is about being mean. So he does not ask, he tells. The second one is the Information Technology genius. He does not communicate, period. So even when he is provided with what he has requested, I never know if he received the material and if he is okay with what I sent. I only hear complaints through the boss when he does not have what he needs. The third young entrepreneur is actually the most promising. He is a good collaborator, and I have made great progress with him, although he disappears for days on end without notifying anyone.

The point I want to make is that there could, and should, be an introductory-level college course for all bright and ambitious students about working collaboratively on any project. The same theories and dynamics apply across all fields. These students would then understand how to propel their talent or genius to even greater heights. Talent without training and experience in the fundamentals of working in a collaborative and strategic fashion can prove wasteful and greatly disappointing to our best and brightest. Time is on the side of the young and they should have the proper foundation before placing themselves and others who have invested in them at risk. Perhaps having delayed the start of their ambitious project until they had more experience in working as a team on less ambitious projects would bring more productive results.

ADVICE FROM BUSINESS SCHOOL DEAN ROBERT SWIERINGA

In response to a series of questions we asked regarding finding your calling, Robert Swieringa, the Dean of the Johnson School of Business at Cornell University for ten years has provided a marvelous set of insights into what is involved in undertaking a graduate business degree from one of the top MBA programs in the country. He also shares in detail the journey he has taken in order to find his calling in life. Virtually all of the key suggestions we have articulated in this guide are reflected in Dean Swieringa's observations and recommendations. There is much sound advice for you to consider here, no matter what your particular fields of interest may be.

Well-educated young adults with predominately liberal arts degrees are a prime target of top MBA programs. Yet these students often are swept into a process that forces choices about career interests without adequate attention and weight given to their personal strengths, interests, and passions.

Most students come to a two-year MBA program with five or more years of business experience and relatively well-defined areas of career interests. The admissions process asks students to indicate their career interests in areas of business (consulting, investment banking, product marketing) for instance, which are then considered and reinforced in correspondence and interviews.

Based on those interests, students are invited to gatherings and other networking events as part of admissions and orientation processes. Career development activities start in earnest in orientation and with increased intensity during the first semester, including corporate presentations, mock interviews, résumé review sessions, and other opportunities to obtain company and industry information and to hone personal skills. Then on-campus interviewing for summer internships begins and continues through early spring, sometimes conflicting with courses and related academic programs. Summer internships are essentially a prolonged interview and evaluation process that plays an increasingly important role in permanent hiring. Recent surveys of Johnson School graduates reveal that they are very positive about the value of their MBA program as a life-changing experience. Graduates highly value what the MBA program will help them achieve, how it helped them grow as individuals, and what they were able to learn.

MY OBSERVATIONS FOR STUDENTS CONSIDERING AN MBA

Follow your passions earlier, not later. An MBA program allows students to obtain knowledge, skills, and perspectives in the functional areas and disciplines of business and in various streams that cut across them (entrepreneurship, leadership, globalization, technology, sustainable enterprise, etc.), and also to identify and pursue their passions. Students are exposed to new ideas, issues, and challenges and find that their passions lie in areas that they may never have considered before. Yet, by engaging in career activities, they may decide to defer following their passions until later. Instead, they often choose to pursue opportunities in popular areas that pay well, to reduce their debt with the hope that they may be able to pursue their passions later. However, these opportunities may not fit with their personal agendas or passions, and soon after graduation they change jobs.

Pursuing opportunities that are not consistent with your personal agendas or passions may result in feelings of remorse and regret. Moreover, you may be less likely to follow your dreams in the future because your personal and professional lives will become increasingly complex over time. You also may become more risk averse over time. I believe that it is easier and less risky to follow your dreams sooner after graduation rather than later.

Students sometimes view the MBA program as a ticket for the first or next job and narrowly focus their selection of courses and related activities. Yet they are unlikely to stay in the same area or with the same organization for their entire professional career—their interests and opportunity sets will change. For example, 2 percent or less of graduates who become consultants or investment bankers will become partners or managing directors and stay with their firms for their professional career. But these opportunities are worth pursuing if they will increase the options and choices that may shape a personally and professionally rewarding career. Students need to stay with these organizations long enough to be effective, as indicated by important promotions, to generate an increasing opportunity set.

It is management and leadership skills that matter. Well-developed quantitative, analytical, and technical skills are necessary for MBAs to get their first or next job, but they are not sufficient for them to keep that job, get the next job, or stay with the organization. Rather, it is their management and leadership skills that will help them keep that job and generate new opportunities. Few MBAs fail because they lack technical skills; rather, they fail because they lack management and leadership skills. Corporate recruiters believe that MBAs generally should develop better people management skills, leadership skills, the ability to make decisions with imperfect information, interpersonal skills, and written communication skills.

I was brought up in a family retail business and worked my way through my undergraduate studies at a small liberal arts college (Augustana College, Rock Island, Illinois) in the Midwest. I majored in economics but took several accounting courses that I enjoyed and found helpful in managing the family business. Upon graduation, I pursued possibilities beyond the family business (career change no. 1), graduated midyear, and was accepted into a graduate program in economics. However, I decided that I would rather pursue professional accounting studies (career change no. 2) and enrolled in an MBA program (Denver) that allowed me to begin graduate work immediately, concentrate in accounting, and also take courses in economics. I was now committed to becoming a partner in a large accounting firm.

About halfway through the MBA program, the head of the accounting department suffered a heart attack and I was asked if I would be willing to teach two accounting courses—one for freshman accounting majors and a second in the evening program. I agreed to teach these courses and so thoroughly enjoyed the experience that it changed my career aspirations and my life. I decided to become an accounting professor (career change no. 3) and entered a Ph.D. program (Illinois), taught two sections of introductory accounting, and continued to run the family business on weekends and during breaks. Where most of my classmates pursued minors in economics and finance, I focused on behavioral science and the behavioral effects of accounting information. I completed my Ph.D. studies and was about to accept an offer from a major university (Iowa) within driving distance of the family business, when I received an inquiry and then an offer from a top business school (Stanford) in California. I accepted the offer and we sold the family business a couple of years later. I then moved to a top business school (Cornell) in the Northeast where I became a tenured full professor engaged in teaching MBAs and executives and writing extensively.

I wrote a series of articles about current accounting issues that attracted attention and triggered an inquiry from the Financial Accounting Standards Board (FASB). I resigned my tenured full professorship to become an accounting standard setter (Member of the Board, FASB) (career change no. 4). After fulfilling the maximum two five-year terms allowed, I returned to academe as a professor at another top business school (Yale) in the Northeast (career change no. 5). At the beginning of my first year at that school, I received an inquiry about the deanship at my previous school in the Northeast (Cornell), which I accepted several months later (career change no. 6). I was dean for ten years, spent part of a sabbatical year at another top school (Harvard), and am now transitioning to being a professor (at Cornell) engaged in teaching MBAs and executives and writing (career change no. 7).

My career reflects how career activities are not a linear process—there are twirls and crinkles and chugs and puffs. It also reflects how passion can be the underlying engine for creating the options and choices that shape a career. It reflects the impact of new options and choices along the way— how one choice begets another, how each position is the means to other opportunities and not an end in itself. Performance in a position generated alternatives that I never anticipated and the importance of being ready to consider new possibilities. At each decision point, there were pressures to stay where I was or continue to do what I was doing. At each decision point, I resisted the pressures to stay put and moved on. I found each change invigorating and stimulating. My career has evolved into ten-plus year segments. I have not stayed in the same activity or position too long. When I returned to academe after my FASB years, I was reinvigorated and stimulated, but I found my academic colleagues who had remained in academe slowing down and losing momentum. The same is now true of my move from the deanship to teaching and research. I am reinvigorated and stimulated by the changes and the prospect of again pursuing my passion with vigor.

TAKE YOUR TIME TO EXPLORE GRADUATE
SCHOOL AND YOUR PASSIONS

We close this chapter with the observation of another highly successful and respected individual who found her calling as a public figure and a major force for social change in an era when women and minorities were discriminated against in employment and educational opportunities. Eleanor Roosevelt said that "the future belongs to those who believe in the beauty of their dreams." Take all the time necessary to conjure up your dream of what your future will be and then follow the necessary steps that will lead you to it.

9

THE MONEY THING

MOST OF US HAVE FACED this concern. How much should money play a role in your career planning? How much is enough? What do you need to feel successful, secure, happy, or appreciated? What kind of lifestyle do you want to maintain or achieve? At some point, we find that almost every student we have worked with confronts "the money thing" and must come to terms with the role of financial compensation in choosing their career or pursuing their calling.

Here are some comments from a young college graduate

who shared with us her growing awareness of the need to balance the pursuit of money and prestige in her career.

MY WHOLE TAKEAWAY FROM THIS year is that you cannot will yourself to be successful doing something that you have no interest in and no passion for. And really, what's the point? You will only be setting yourself up for failure. Every job should help you grow as a person and get closer to the best professional version of yourself. The key is to find something that you want to think about when you're away from the office, not something that gives you panic attacks in the middle of a dinner with friends. I am so over the idea that the only respectable profession involves being a cog in a wheel at a large, prestigious bank, law firm, etc. Everyone should pursue a career in an area that they want to learn more about and that they are genuinely interested in. No matter what your previous track record, you cannot feign interest or passion for 60-plus hours a week; it will get you absolutely nowhere ... except maybe on the couch of a shrink. You will only be successful if you do what you love.

As someone who made the absolute worst career decisions possible, I think the key is that college students need to know ALL of their options, and this requires being proactive ... not just listening to the advice of parents, mentors, etc., but actually sitting down and thinking about your strengths, your interests, where you would like to be in ten years, etc., and then using resources, such as career counselors and parents to help you figure out steps.

For example, if you are someone like me whose eye jumps immediately to anything fashion-, retail-, or sports-related in the newspaper, and then moves to business and world affairs, that should be an indication that those are the areas in which you should pursue a career. If your eye immediately jumps to the business section, you probably won't find too much fulfillment being an artist.

It's okay to start a career in a "less serious field," provided you work your butt off and get the job done well. You cannot go to someone and say, "Help me figure out what I should do with my life," because only you can answer that question. A job should be something that gives you a sense of accomplishment and fulfillment, not something that strips you of your confidence, your dignity, or your will to live. I have found in my own personal experience that you will never be able to make the right decision if you do not know who you are. This self-knowledge and self-reflection are absolutely vital. If you do not take these steps, you will likely end up losing a year of experience to someone who has taken these steps.

The most important part of the career search process is not acing the interview for the most high-status job, but rather determining what it is that will make you happy. Because life and work are to be enjoyed. And, for most people, it takes more than a big paycheck and a "prestigious" business card to achieve professional happiness and fulfillment.

BALANCING MONEY AND LIFESTYLE

While money plays some role in almost every career decision, it is more important to some individuals than others. Today, surveys show that many college students and graduates are also very concerned with other "lifestyle" issues, including how much time they will spend on their job, how much they can balance that with time for their family, and how they will continue to be able to pursue recreational activities and social life. Additionally, social and environmental concerns have become more important to many college students and graduates of this generation. Considering an employer's record on sustainability issues, human rights concerns, or fair employment practices tops many job seekers' lists of priorities.

How much is your path being driven by money? Do you need to consider delaying some income today in order to earn credentials, pay your dues in an entry-level job, or gain experience through an internship? What other lifestyle concerns will be important to you in creating your job and living environment? As many grim-faced salary men in their fifties or sixties will tell you, a big paycheck does not often turn out to be much solace for innumerable hours spent away from family and friends, high-stress traveling around the country or the world, or a high-stress, high-stakes work environment.

If money is important to you, and earning a certain amount of discretionary income is key to your life satisfaction, then you should indeed factor this into your career planning. Perhaps you feel a need to maintain the same (or higher) standard of living as your parents. Material goods might interest you to the point that you will not be fulfilled without the chance to purchase them and live a more plush lifestyle. You know what? That's okay. You just need to be honest with yourself about that and recognize the potential sacrifices you might make along the way. Making partner in a law firm takes a huge amount of dedication and time. When you get there, you'll have landed a fairly secure and lucrative position.

Trading securities can earn you serious bonuses at the end of the year. But the culture of the trading floor is not for everyone. Remember that Ivy League graduate who found herself the only woman among a clique of highly competitive, sexist, ill-mannered guys? She needed only a year to figure out she was in the wrong environment. There was a lot of money on the table for her if she stayed, but she knew the sacrifices weren't worth it.

Had she stuck around for a few years, she probably would have witnessed many of her colleagues losing their jobs as economic cycles or new directors came and went. In this current climate, we are again seeing many highly educated and successful business people looking for work. A willingness to move around the United States or abroad comes with the territory if you want to find your way back into the fold.

You might be one of the many young people today who

look at the very rich professionals out there—hedge fund managers, brokers, real estate developers, law partners, corporate CEOs, and the like—who make up the top 1 percent of income brackets, and envision yourself among their ranks. You might get there, but doing so will take a lot of hard work and a lot of personal sacrifices. Just ask anyone in these positions. It will also take a bit of luck, the serendipity of being at the right place at the right time—getting a job at the right hedge fund, new Internet startup, or corporate Cinderella story. Make sure to ask yourself if the sacrifices are worth it, and whether you'll be okay if your first or second or fifth attempts to climb the ladder or strike it rich don't pan out.

One lesson we have imparted repeatedly to those we have counseled is not to overlook the traditional industry paths even as new phenomena take centerstage in our national attention. Consider the many paths to success and potential security—often money is a proxy for security—to be found in major corporations. Look at the Fortune 500 and beyond for careers in companies like General Electric, Johnson & Johnson, United Illuminating, Boeing, John Deere. Yes you'll find a lot of action and growth potential at companies like Google, Intel, Yahoo!, and Facebook, as well as innumerable other Web-based companies. Giants like Microsoft and Apple have much to offer graduates with business, technical, and other expertise. Yet companies like Dow Chemical, General Motors, and Pfizer are looking for medical, technical, engineering, business, and just plain smart liberal arts graduates as well.

CHOOSING A PLACE TO LIVE

Your generation is by any measure the most mobile, global, and flexible yet. You truly do have the choice to live anywhere you want, to do anything you want, to change your mind anytime your want. You have and will develop a network through online community building which you can maintain for a lifetime. Moving from Cleveland to Seattle to New York will not require you to drop your community of friends or business acquaintances. You will not need to spend one or more days each week corresponding by letter with them.

This is in many ways perplexing and daunting for many of you. With so many choices, how should you choose? Clearly your family and hometown will exert some geographical pull on you. Your eventual spouse or life partner will also have some say in this choice. Your first job offer could pull you in a direction you never imagined. We do find that many young graduates we speak with will begin some of their career planning by making very clear statements about where they do and do not want to live.

Perhaps you are hoping to move out West to someplace fun and young and outdoorsy. You've always wanted to live in New York, or San Francisco, or Los Angeles, or Miami. These are places with fun young scenes and a lot going on. Many want to return to their roots in or near such an environment, while others want to get as far away from home as possible. If you like the area where you attended college, you might never leave, particularly if there are some career connections you have built up there. Graduate school could be another geographic curveball.

Now hear this: If you want to be successful in certain careers, you are going to have to be flexible in terms of where you live. If geography is your most important consideration, and you absolutely must live in one particular region or city, then you'd better plan for a career that will allow you to do that. You could be a doctor, psychologist, architect, physical therapist, or teacher, for example, and locate your practice in one place. That is doable. But certain careers, such as banking, the foreign service, corporate management, human resources work, or consulting, will likely require substantial travel during your career and a willingness either to take a new posting when one is offered in order to move up the corporate ladder, or, as noted above, an ability to move to a new city to find work if you have lost your current job.

SEE MONEY AS A NECESSARY BUT NOT SUFFICIENT FACTOR

We all need money to survive, to take care of our family, to build security. You might have student loans to repay, medical bills to handle, a mortgage to finance. Money (aka a well-paying job) is necessary to help you manage all these things. But everyone, and we truly believe this, requires more. A big

paycheck is not sufficient to bring you contentment or fulfillment. Within the range of careers with high income potential, there are a lot of choices and variations. You can balance
what kind of legal, finance, architecture, or engineering career you want. You can choose to work for a large corporate
firm or a small-town practice. You can work for someone else,
or work for yourself. You can live in a major metropolitan
area with a high cost of living or move to a smaller middle-
American town or city where you can buy a lot more house
on a modest salary.

As with fame, prestige, industry leadership, and other
forms of nonfinancial recognition, the money thing can be-
guile you. Be explicit and honest with yourself and your advisers about your needs in these areas.

10

BUILDING VALUES INTO YOUR CAREER

How important are values to you in your work? How much does your work need to have "meaning"? Some of the career, personality type, and interest evaluations, such as the Myers-Briggs Type Indicator, can help you establish what role a values orientation might play in your work life. We have found this distinction to be a critical factor in making career decisions for many college students and graduates today. For those whose Thread involves a strong "making a difference" element, choosing a job without that orientation can lead to extraordinary dissatisfaction.

UNDERSTANDING YOUR VALUES

Social scientists and philosophers spend lifetimes debating differences between values, ethics, morals, and other ways of discerning meaning in what matters to us as individuals. For some, a values system might be strongly based in your religious faith. Such a strong element of spirituality grounded in a particular religious tradition might be the core of your beliefs about what is right and wrong, and what is important to you in finding purpose and meaning in your life. It might be essential for you to find a calling that allows you to express your religious beliefs through your life's work. You might be truly "called" to serve others in some fashion, through a form of religious ministry, through social work, or through teaching, counseling, or volunteering in your community.

Others find values in a spiritual or nonspiritual way, and develop a strong moral code not explicitly connected to a religious tradition. You might not belong to a particular religious community, but you can have strongly held convictions about human rights, the environment, making a difference in the lives of others, animal rights, civil rights, or social and economic equality. Just as you face the money thing in your search for a calling and career, you will at some point in time face "the values thing."

It is possible, perhaps even likely, that other than basic ethical standards of practice, values are not important to you in your vocation. You could fulfill your interest in making a difference in your community or the world at large through avocational pursuits. No community in this country would function effectively without the donations of time, expertise, and resources from those working in jobs and industries not explicitly focused on helping others, or those retired from these positions. In some cases, senior executives find a second or third career in their mid or late life working in a volunteer, nonprofit, or governmental capacity.

Whether you choose to pursue a career with a strong values orientation—say, working for a company that cleans up toxic waste sites, counseling abused and neglected children, or fighting poverty in developing countries—or not, you should also consider the kinds of values that are important to you in your workplace. Even among profit-oriented businesses that do not have a "helping" or "ministering" ethos as their main focus—working for a major oil company, car manufacturer, or financial institution, for example—you will find variations in terms of how strongly the industry and individual employers emphasize such values as civility, non-discrimination and fair employment practices, affirmative action, sustainability, family leave policies, ethical business practices, giving back through corporate donations or community service activities, or other conservative, liberal, religious, or nonreligious values that might be important to you.

For Juilliard president Joseph Polisi, what mattered was excellence in the arts and community service.

THE ELEMENTS THAT MATTERED TO me most in deciding what professional path I would pursue were the desire
to experience excellence in my professional endeavors and
my hope to have my work ultimately have a positive impact
on individuals and society. As a result, I am constantly evaluating the quality of the educational and artistic programs
at Juilliard and often find myself saying to community
members that "we are as good as our last performance." In
addition, I have asked faculty members and administrators
to develop programs at Juilliard that emphasize "community outreach" so that the young artists (our students) understand that they have a responsibility to "give back" to a
community outside of Juilliard through their art. Our students have embraced this philosophy over the years, so that
in 2009 a majority of Juilliard students are involved in some
type of outreach activity.

The stories of other professionals we have included in the
book also offer many suggestions about the importance of
giving back through their work or in addition to their work.

If you are strongly oriented toward furthering certain
values, and working in an environment or for a company
that maintains and promotes them, then make sure you do
your research on career paths as well as different organizations within these fields. Match your own self-knowledge
with what you can learn so that you can make the best short-
and long-term match possible.

IDENTIFYING VALUES-ORIENTED PROFESSIONS

In the for-profit sector, there are professions that allow you to wear your values on your sleeve more visibly. Certainly the helping professions of medicine, psychology, nursing, public health, psychiatry and psychology, counseling, social work, physical therapy, dentistry, optometry, and so on will fit this profile. Within the educational sphere, teaching, administration, tutoring, special education services, school social work, and school psychology allow you to impact students from early ages through young adulthood. A faith-based profession, from the ministry to pastoral counseling to serving as a chaplain in a school or the armed forces would allow you to pursue your calling from a religious or spiritual perspective. Serving your country in the armed forces as a career officer would provide you with a number of ways to make a difference and promote your values and those of the country.

In a number of these professions, you will likely find your career consisting of a variety of jobs, jobs that vacillate between for-profit and not-for-profit enterprises, including governmental and nongovernmental organizations. A private practice physician, for example, might work for a nonprofit health-care provider serving lower-income families; take a post at the Centers for Disease Control working in a governmental capacity; or join with an international organization like Save the Children (a U.S.-based nonprofit) or Doctors Without Borders or UNICEF. A psychologist or social worker might maintain a private practice while also working with a local counseling or family services agency to provide therapy on a sliding fee scale.

The lines between for-profit, not-for-profit (those 501.c.3 organizations you often hear about, for example), and governmental organizations are blurring in many respects, though with some significant differences among these groups. In this fast-growing and highly diverse universe, you will find a lot of interesting opportunities and the chance to pursue your passions and your values in multiple ways.

UNDERSTANDING NOT-FOR-PROFIT ORGANIZATIONS

Winston Churchill once said: "We make a living by what we get. We make a life by what we give." There are three major enterprises that are concerned with societal issues:

- Not-for-profit organizations, such as most schools and colleges, hospitals, social welfare organizations, religious institutions, cultural arts organizations, service organizations like the Red Cross and Ameri-Cares, and advocacy organizations like the Nature Conservancy and NAACP.

- Public sector or governmental organizations, such as local, state, and federal governmental agencies, libraries, and international governmental and nongovernmental organizations.

- For-profit entities that have a social mission and/or a nonprofit foundation within their organization, such as Target, Ben & Jerry's, Tom's of Maine, Johnson & Johnson, and Mary Kay.

The not-for-profit sector of the American economy now includes nearly 1.5 million organizations that spend $500 billion each year. Approximately 6 percent of all U.S. organizations are not-for-profit. One in fifteen Americans work for a nonprofit organization, comprising 10 percent of the workforce, and accounting for 7 percent of the gross national product.

> The Federal government posts more than 15,000 different kinds of jobs, ranging from economist to summer intern on its Web site, www.usajobs.opm.gov

PROFITING FROM NOT-FOR-PROFITS

Why are more college graduates considering positions in the multitude of nonprofit and public service organizations today? What are the kinds of opportunities available outside the for-profit sector? Can you do well by doing good?

First, here are some comments from a career professional who has contributed to both the profit and nonprofit sectors. Curt Welling spent almost three decades working in investment banking. Today he leads AmeriCares, a major U.S. not-for-profit agency sponsoring relief work around the world. Here are Welling's recent comments to the graduating class at Dartmouth's Tuck School of Business.

ONE OF THE QUESTIONS I am most frequently asked is this: What is the biggest difference between the "for-profit" and "nonprofit" worlds? While there are many facets to this question, and, at the risk of oversimplifying, I would characterize it this way: The perspective of the "for-profit" world is the perspective of the *marketplace*. The perspective of the "nonprofit" world is the perspective of the *mission*.

What are the implications of this difference in perspective? The "for-profit" world tends to be all about competition—for both resources and customers—and about efficiency, productivity, and returns; about winning, often without regard to the human consequences, or recently without regard to moral implications. Much of this focus is precisely as it should be. Some is clearly not.

The "nonprofit" world tends to be all about humanity and compassion: about service, about impacts and outcomes; about morality; about human consequences. And almost always without regard to personal compensation: Every person at AmeriCares walks through the door each day knowing they could make more money doing something else.

Unfortunately, too many nonprofits also operate without regard to efficiency, financial implications, and the financial environment.

The bottom line, however, is this: Neither of these perspectives is a sufficient condition for long-term success. Neither is the "right" perspective. Each can learn from the other, and each lesson is important.

There has been a rise in community service involvement in high school, college, and beyond, and this volunteerism has played a role in helping many people identify and hone major interests and skills.

If you have devoted yourself to service in your early years and through college, you might find a fulfilling and secure career by establishing yourself in a service-oriented position in a nonprofit organization, or perhaps through other forms of socially conscious entrepreneurship. Public service and government entities are other places to find great career opportunities.

FORGIVE THOSE LOANS: I'M SERVING THE PUBLIC!

The College Cost Reduction and Access Act of 2007 increases the opportunities for students to eliminate student loan debt by working in certain fields after graduating college. If you work for ten years in a qualified public service position, your Stafford, PLUS, and federal consolidation loans (principal and interest accrued) through the Department of Education's Direct Loan program can be forgiven. If you have nondirect loans, you can consolidate them through the Direct Loan program in order to qualify for the loan forgiveness plan.

If you are working in a lower-paying field (and, yes, that typically includes public and nonprofit service jobs), you can choose to pay your loans through the income-contingent repayment plan, which ties your payments during the ten-year repayment period to your current income. As long as you make those regular payments for ten years while working in a qualifying field, the remainder of your debt will be erased.

Which jobs qualify? Public service jobs, including local, state, and federal government jobs like law enforcement, firefighting, teaching, or military service. Also, some nonprofit employees, emergency services workers, lawyers working in public interest law, librarians, Tribal College faculty, social workers, and health and child-care workers. See the Department's Web site for more information on these and other loan forgiveness opportunities: www.studentaid.ed.gov/students/attachments/siteresources/LoanForgivenessMarch18.pdf

Following the federal lead, Tufts University announced its own loan-forgiveness plans for Tufts students and alumni who work in certain public service and nonprofit careers. In an example of a for-profit entrepreneur making a difference in another way, the funds to begin the program come from the Omidyar-Tufts Microfinance Fund, established by a $100 million gift to Tufts from alumnus Pierre Omidyar, the founder of eBay, and his wife, Pamela, also a graduate of Tufts.

CARRIE TATE'S STORY

Carrie, a young graduate of Dickinson College, shared her motivational story with us. Her story demonstrates the importance of many of the concepts we have outlined and the extraordinary rewards you can receive by pursuing a service-oriented career.

I WASN'T ALWAYS SURE WHAT I wanted to do with my life beyond high school. I skipped back and forth between ideas of teaching in elementary school, writing, and finding a career that involved working with kids. I came to college thinking I would major in psychology and look into the teacher certification program that my college offered, and I thought perhaps I would continue to pursue a master's degree right after college. Plans changed for me when I got to college and didn't find myself very engaged in the psychology courses I was taking. I tried more than one class in the department my first year and none of them really clicked for me. Panicking, I went to my adviser who suggested that I try out classes in some other departments just to see if anything else caught my interest. I sampled classes in religion, sociology, and American studies.

I was immediately hooked on American studies after taking a class called Mass Media. I liked the idea of studying American culture—history, music, race, gender, class, and social structures—a little bit of everything that interested me. My American studies major was one of the Threads that influenced me to pursue a career working in the community, because I learned so much about inequality and stratification and social change in our nation's history. I was learning about this detailed portrait of American life and American culture through the wide variety of classes I was taking, and I wanted to learn more about American culture by getting my feet wet and working directly within the community with other people to learn more about relationships, poverty and wealth, traditions, and everything else that interested me about families in America.

I got involved in a job with an after-school program while in college, joined a co-ed national service fraternity, and started looking for ways to stay involved in the community over the summer. During my sophomore year, I found the perfect opportunity to channel my passions when I found the Institute on Philanthropy and Voluntary Service, which has a two-month-long summer program that places students with nonprofit internships while offering classes about American society and the nonprofit sector. I came away from that summer experience with so many different ideas about what I wanted to do next, but I was sure that I wanted to work within the nonprofit sector in an education-related field.

The more I got involved in my community, the more I knew I wanted to create change and serve and work with/ help people who didn't have the same advantages as I had. I realized more and more how blessed I was to have been living such a comfortable life where I was practically handed everything I needed and wanted. I felt a pressing need to give and provide and serve. I wanted to find a career that would be meaningful to me, that would have a lasting impact, and that would help me to continue to grow and change as a person while I helped others.

Before I knew it, I was starting my senior year of college. I was completely unsure of what I wanted to do after college and felt a lot of pressure as most of my friends were studying for the GRE and applying to graduate schools. I knew that grad school wasn't the right next step for me, because I had no idea what I would study. When I told them I was interested in a career in the nonprofit sector, a few people suggested I look into master's programs in public administration or public affairs. I looked into several programs, many of which are still of interest to me, but I didn't feel comfortable putting so much money toward more education when I wasn't one hundred percent sure that it was *exactly* what I wanted to do. I still had so many unanswered questions. The nonprofit sector was huge. Where would I work? What issues did I want to support or change or confront?

Some members of the Peace Corps came to my college to talk about their experiences and recruit new applicants. I started researching domestic programs that offered a similar service experience. I came across AmeriCorps National Civilian Community Corps (NCCC), and one of my roommates put me in touch with a friend who had recently completed the program. I was completely sold. I applied for

AmeriCorps NCCC and was accepted, and I began the ten-month team-based national service program in October 2007. Over the course of the next ten months, I saw the country and found myself face to face with people in the communities where my team was placed who needed my help the most. I worked with an environmental conservation organization in Nevada and northern Arizona, I built houses while working with two Habitat branches along the coast of Mississippi and in southern Louisiana, and I weatherized people's homes while installing energy/environmentally friendly and efficient lightbulbs and teaching them about conservation.

I met people, listened to their stories about Hurricane Katrina, about family, about poverty, about change. My experiences opened my eyes to so many more areas where I could see myself working and broadened my interests. I no longer viewed education and kids as the sole keywords for my job search, but rather I found myself adding the environment, sustainable energy, affordable housing, policy, and hunger/homelessness to my areas of interest. My Thread had taken me to AmeriCorps NCCC, which gave me a whole new perspective on the country where I lived and the ways in which I could create change, make a difference, and have a lasting impact.

I am in the middle of a job-search for my next adventure. I am still only twenty-two years old, and I have so many years ahead of me to do *so* much. I am taking the experiences I had over the last year and using them to help me seek out employment opportunities within the nonprofit sector that will match some of my interests. While some of my friends are successfully taking on their graduate program work, others are making salaries I might never see in the line of work I am pursuing, but I am okay with all of that. For *me,* this was the right path. I learned to let go of whatever pressures I felt from my peers or my family. As I am in the process of making some incredibly difficult life decisions right now, trying to get my first job in the "real world," my passion to serve my community and create change are at the front of my mind.

The best advice I can give is to find your passion, whatever it may be, and let that passion direct you in whatever career you pursue. I know so many people who have let other factors influence their life decisions, and they don't necessarily end up happy in whatever they are doing. Look at your skills, figure out what drives you and motivates you and makes you tick, and try to look for careers that will harness your skills and your drive together. And if you find yourself graduating from college and you're really unsure of where to go next, I would advise taking time to figure out the next step rather than rushing into something or throwing yourself out on the job market with no direction. It's hard to do something every day that you don't really enjoy, and my opinion is that there is no rush to jump into the real world before you are ready. If you haven't figured out what your passion is, try new things, force yourself to get involved in your community, and consider your options.

THERE ARE SO MANY WAYS
TO MAKE A DIFFERENCE

How can you bring your values to the forefront and make a difference? An interest in sustainability, education, health care, or public service, for example, could lead to successful involvements in new or existing cause-oriented organizations or governmental institutions. For some, nonprofit or public service work is a second or third career choice, after having explored banking, law, or some other profit-oriented career. You might teach for a lifetime at an elementary school, high school, college, or graduate school. These could include public as well as independent and parochial schools, boarding and day schools, American and international schools.

How do nonprofits come into existence? Typically, a creative and entrepreneurial individual pursues his or her big idea and finds the funding to start an organization to solve a big problem, serve a need, or promote a cause. You might start your own organization, seeking like-minded individuals to join with you, and putting your own money on the table. Just as likely, you'll need to identify patrons, including individuals willing to provide seed money and continuing support, as well as foundations and governmental grant-making institutions.

Consider the inspiring example of Greg Mortenson, a climber who almost died attempting to summit K2 in central Asia. Rescued by a local guide and resuscitated in a local village, he became committed to returning to northern Pakistan to provide schools and basic resources to the local villagers, particularly the girls who had little or no access to formal schooling. Mortenson returned many times, and with the support of key individual funders, he started both the Central Asia Institute and the Pennies for Peace program (www .ikat.org) to raise money to support his education efforts in Afghanistan and Pakistan. His book *Three Cups of Tea* illustrates how a small idea and commitment can become a big idea and a life's calling.

From new and small-scale organizations like Mortenson's to well-established national and international nonprofits like Save the Children, the Red Cross, the Salvation Army, or the Sierra Club, you might find a group that already represents your ideal fit, your place to fulfill your calling. There are thousands of foundations and grant-making organizations, from small family foundations to huge institutions like the Rockefeller, Ford, Gates, or Carnegie foundations. They need bright, well-educated liberal arts graduates to promote their missions, write RFPs (Requests for Proposals) and evaluate them, network with funders and funds seekers, and provide management, operations, and budgetary assistance. You could find yourself using your writing skills to write RFPs for a major foundation. You could use your people and communications skills to work as a development officer to raise money for a nonprofit. You could use your quantitative skills as a Chief Financial Officer or Treasurer. Management skills? Why not be a CEO or president of a nonprofit or governmental institution?

Legal skills? You can work as an in-house counsel or member of a pro-bono partnership providing free or low-cost legal services to nonprofit organizations.

The key is understanding that you can develop a professional, challenging, and, depending on the organization and your level of responsibility within it, potentially lucrative and financially secure career within the not-for-profit world. You can do well by doing good. You can perform essential public and community service work, maintain and promote your values orientation, and find good benefits and compensation that just might provide the lifestyle that suits you.

11

FINDING YOUR CALLING

> And only the Master shall praise us, and only the Master shall blame;
> And no one shall work for money, and no one shall work for fame;
> But each for the joy of the working, and each, in his separate star,
> Shall draw the Thing as he sees It, for the God of Things as They Are!
>
> —RUDYARD KIPLING, "L'ENVOI"

WHAT IS A CALLING? DOES everyone have one? More than one? Have you discovered one by pursuing your Thread? How do you know it when you see it?

We have used the word *calling* a lot through this book, sometimes interchangeably with *career*. Yet to most people, these are two distinct concepts. Ideally, as you follow your Threads through your life, you will be able to match up your career and your calling as closely as possible.

Max Weber, the legendary sociologist, introduced the idea of the calling to the modern world in the early twentieth century in his classic work, *The Protestant Ethic and the Spirit of Capitalism*. In seeking to explain the rise of capitalism and why it occurred first in Western Europe, Weber argued that there was a unique connection between market-driven capitalism with its division of labor and some of the concepts inherent in and resulting from, sometimes quite unintentionally, the teachings of the Protestant reformers. The shift from an otherworldly focus to an emphasis on doing God's work in the material world begins with Martin Luther and the Reformation, and was particularly expanded upon by John Calvin and John Knox.

Weber identified a calling as "a religious conception, that of a task set by God . . . the fulfillment of duty in worldly affairs as the highest form which the moral activity of the individual could assume." Calvinism further established connections between capitalist work efforts, or, more broadly, hard work in one's life work, through the doctrine of predestination. Paradoxically, this notion that one was chosen by God to be one of the "elect," destined for salvation, furthered efforts on the part of individuals to prove that they were so. Protestantism advised the faithful to find their calling and to work as hard as they could in it. At the same time, asceticism, including an emphasis on saving and living frugally and modestly, supported the beginnings of capital accumulation. Those who succeeded in their livelihood believed that they were seeing signs of their own predestined salvation and lived with the conviction that they were one of God's chosen.

It is primarily through this conception of calling that we

see a religious basis for the idea. Weber pointed to the predominantly Anglo-Saxon roots of the idea, and the connections between Protestantism and the development of modern capitalism. Today, some continue to imbue the idea of a calling with a religious foundation, a life's purpose as ordained by God or at least some higher power. Some go further to identify a calling as purely a religious involvement. That is, one is called to serve God in one's work, through ministry, missionary work, or religious education, for example.

Others have broadened the idea of a calling, and decoupled the idea from its religious connotations. Calling can thus be understood in more secular or humanistic terms. *Merriam-Webster's Collegiate Dictionary,* for example, offers both definitions of *calling:*

> 1: a strong inner impulse toward a particular course of action especially when accompanied by conviction of divine influence
>
> 2: the vocation or profession in which one customarily engages

The word *vocation* is similarly complicated by both religious and more modern secular meanings. Here is *Merriam-Webster's* definition of *vocation,* which is derived from Latin words meaning *summons* or *call:*

> 1 a: a summons or strong inclination to a particular state or course of action; especially : a divine call to the religious life

b: an entry into the priesthood or a religious order

2 a: the work in which a person is regularly employed : occupation b: the persons engaged in a particular occupation

3: the special function of an individual or group

If vocation and calling are roughly synonymous, at least in today's usage, then it will be more helpful to distinguish between these terms and the word *avocation*. Here is the definition from *Merriam-Webster's,* derived from the Latin word meaning *to call away*:

1 archaic : diversion, distraction

2: customary employment : vocation

3: a subordinate occupation pursued in addition to one's vocation especially for enjoyment : hobby

How do you distinguish an avocation from a vocation? When is it best to develop your interest into a career, as opposed to keeping it as a passionate pursuit that is not your main form of earning a living?

These are some of the central questions of this book and certainly vital to your own reflections about deciding on a career plan or discovering your calling. One way to approach this is to consider whether your avocation or avocations are primarily distractions and diversions—playing tennis or poker on the weekends, participating in a book club, enjoying movies or video games, volunteering as a mentor, participating in your church or synagogue as a deacon or religious educator—

or represent significant "subordinate occupations" or hobbies that could conceivably become your primary source of employment and income.

We have a friend who began life after college as an advertising and marketing professional. He commuted every day to New York City on the train, using his writing and creative skills to develop ad campaigns. Like many aspiring authors and casual writers, he began to write the proverbial "book on the train." Except in this case he managed to secure an agent, who helped him secure a publisher. After his first book hit the market and did reasonably well, he landed a second contract. This gave him the confidence to quit his day job and follow his dream of writing full-time. He took some local office space and joined the virtual world. He now writes every day, including as a coauthor with a bestselling fiction writer, and has the daily lifestyle with his family for which he had hoped.

We have seen instances of amateur photographers and videographers opening studios catering to sports, family photography, or animals; musicians making the transition to professional work, through private teaching, performance and touring, or playing for children's parties; passionate cooks becoming private chefs and nutritionists or teaching local classes and leading tours of culinary sites in the U.S. and abroad; athletes becoming personal trainers or physical therapists; fashionistas opening boutiques, making crafts to be sold from their houses, or consulting; interior decorators; recreational therapists; travel agents!

At the same time, there are a lot of hobbyists out there pursuing their avocational passions on the side while they maintain a day job that is more traditional—how about those musician bankers, doctors, and lawyers; chef advertising directors; triathalon techies; card-playing investment managers; skiing ministers? Each of us must find our own balance, an equilibrium that can shift over time as we enter and leave various life stages. As we hope you have learned by now, the important thing is to be aware of creating that balance and to do so in a considered way.

APPENDIX

ADDITIONAL CAREER PLANNING RESOURCES

Occupational Outlook Handbook, Annual
www.bls.gov/OCO

Dictionary of Occupational Titles
www.occupationalinfo.org

Moody's Industry Review
www.economy.com/home/products

Plunkett's Almanac of American Employers
www.plunkettresearch.com

SOURCES FOR INTERNSHIPS AND VOLUNTEER OPPORTUNITIES

AmeriCorps
www.americorps.org

ACCESS: Networking in the Public Interest
www.communityjobs.org

Action Without Borders
www.idealist.org

American Red Cross
www.redcross.org

Big Brothers/Big Sisters
www.bigbrothersbigsisters.org

Boy Scouts of America/Girl Scouts of America
www.scouting.org, www.girlscouts.org

Boys & Girls Clubs of America
www.bgca.org

Campus Outreach Opportunity League
www.cool2serve.org

Habitat For Humanity
www.habitat.org

Learn and Serve Clearinghouse
www.servicelearning.org

National Center for Youth Law
www.youthlaw.org

National Urban League
www.nul.org

YMCA, YWCA
www.ymca.net, www.ywca.org

ADDITIONAL WEB SITES

Internships:
www.internshipprograms.com

Volunteering:
www.4laborsoflove.org

Nonprofits, activism, government service:
www.essential.org/links and www.usajobs.opm.gov

Companies to research:
www.wetfeet.com and www.hoovers.com

Fortune Magazine
www.fortune.com
Careers section has lots of helpful information on job hunting. Includes model cover letters, résumés, networking, interviewing, relevant articles.

Richard Bolles's *Parachute* work online:
www.jobhuntersbible.com
Includes links to helpful Web sites.

Holland's Self Directed Search
www.self-directed-search.com
John Holland's SDS classifies individuals into six categories and matches with appropriate careers.

The Career Key:
www.ncsu.edu/careerkey
Provides a free version of Holland's SDS thanks to North Carolina State University.